Lessons
IN Tolerance
AND Diversity

Susanna Palomares

INNERCHOICE Publishing
15079 Oak Chase Court
Wellington, FL 33414

www.InnerchoicePublishing.com

Cover: Dave Cowan

Editor: Dianne Schilling

ISBN - 10: 1-56499-057-0

ISBN - 13: 978-1-56499-057-0

INNERCHOICE Publishing
15079 Oak Chase Court
Wellington, FL 33414

www.InnerchoicePublishing.com

Contents

Thank You . . .

Special thanks for making valuable recommendations to the development of this book go to Dr. Keith Ward and the teacher/graduate students in his class on Classroom Diversity at East Stroudsburg University:

Tara Buskirk	Denise Casey
Bobbi Jo Cuvo	Charles Falteich
Carol Free	Victoria Milburn
Dana Morgan	Nicole Palkovic
Dawn Seiple	

Thanks also for help, ideas, and research to Terri Akin, Cristina Casanova, Dr. James W. Cole, David Cowan, Sue Finney, David Irving, Robert Miles, and Nanci Willson; to Laurie Beth Jones for her books and seminars that embody the essence of tolerance and from which I learn so much; and to Cathrine Kellison for endless hours of discussion on this topic and for the inspiration she always ignites. And to Bradley and Cathy Winch for being my wonderful and tolerant partners.

Thanks always to Dianne Schilling for being the eternally great editor and for always being willing to brainstorm, discuss, banter, and generally help me to clarify my thoughts.

Finally, I give a special note of recognition to the Fourth Lake Community for living tolerance every day.

> *How wonderful it is that nobody need wait a single moment before starting to improve the world.*
>
> Anne Frank

Lessons in Tolerance and Diversity
Introduction and Theory

Our society — and our schools — grow more extraordinarily varied and complex with each passing day. While more children from diverse racial, ethnic and cultural backgrounds are attending schools, the reception they encounter does not always reflect the highest democratic values and traditions of our nation. Schools, which are often more diverse than the neighborhoods from which their students come, are becoming hotbeds of racial strife and conflict.

We must make concerted efforts to lessen racial conflict and encourage more harmony among our increasingly diverse youth. Schools need to take proactive steps to promote understanding and tolerance, and to help students appreciate, rather than fear, people different from themselves.

The 1995 Declaration of Principles on Tolerance, proclaimed and signed by the member states of the United Nations Educational Scientific and Cultural Organization (UNESCO) states:

> *Education for tolerance should be considered an urgent imperative: that is why it is necessary to promote systematic and national tolerance teaching methods that will address the cultural, social, economic, political and religious sources of intolerance — major roots of violence and exclusion. Education policies and programs should contribute to development of understanding, solidarity and tolerance among individuals as well as among ethnic, social, cultural, religious and linguistic groups and nations.*

Lessons in Tolerance and Diversity is designed to aid individual teachers, counselors, and others to respond to this mandate. When used as part of a comprehensive prejudice-reduction program, its benefits are multiplied. The purpose of the book is to provide educators with tools to help reduce racial, religious, ethnic and social prejudice in our schools and to promote tolerance and the celebration of diversity among our children.

Major Concepts Related to Tolerance and Diversity

Tolerance is almost a buzzword these days, a linguistic symbol for a virtue sorely needed and sometimes pitifully lacking in our society. To tolerate something means to allow it, without prohibition or opposition. A doctor who asks if you can tolerate a particular medicine wants to know if your body will accept it without reaction or rejection. In the parlance of human relations tolerance implies acceptance and something more — underlying respect.

Having tolerance for another person or group of people means respecting differences, being able to think or say, "You and I are different. We look, sound, and think differently. We don't agree on everything and that's okay."

Tolerance implies the willingness to open oneself to new information. Openness allows us to gather the input necessary to break down stereotypes. One way to become more tolerant is to consciously push out on the boundaries of our individual comfort zone. Expansion of our comfort zone is a step beyond openness and implies a determination to grow.

Research has shown that tolerance involves the ability to change our minds, something open-minded and growth-minded people are comfortable doing. In one experiment, people who had been assessed as either tolerant or intolerant were shown a stack of drawings in which a picture of a cat was slowly transformed into a picture of a dog. When asked to identify each drawing, tolerant people started off with "cat," answered "I don't know" during the altered drawings, and concluded with "dog." Intolerant people insisted that the drawing was a cat even when it was indecipherable.

Diversity is just another word for differences. People possess different qualities, characteristics, values, beliefs and habits. Valuing diversity means embracing those differences, in effect saying, "I can benefit from being around people who are different from me. I want to learn from their ideas and values and am enriched by the exposure."

Diversity is not restricted to racial differences. It includes ethnic and cultural differences, ability differences, social and economic differences and religious differences. Intolerance of diversity takes many forms, among them racism, sexism, ageism, anti-Semitism, ethnic bigotry and homophobia.

Stereotypes are the *cognitive* component of intolerance — products of thought and belief systems. A stereotype is an oversimplified generalization about an entire group of people without regard for individual differences. We all generalize, fitting new ideas and information into convenient groupings in order to more easily make judgments and decisions. Vegetables are good for you. Desserts are sweet. However, even positive stereotypes applied to humans — "Asians are good students," "Blacks are talented athletes" — can have a negative impact.

Prejudice is the *affective* component of intolerance. Prejudice by definition excludes reason — it's *pre*-judging based on an emotional response, and is often deeply embedded and difficult to change. The prejudiced person is predisposed to respond in a particular way — usually negative — regardless of the facts.

Discrimination is the *behavioral* component of intolerance — the acting out of prejudice. On the basis of our stereotyped thoughts and prejudiced feelings we treat others unfairly or deny them justice. We ignore, degrade, exclude, isolate, reject, exploit, persecute, victimize and subjugate.

Seeds of Intolerance

Prejudice and intolerance are complex phenomena, and no single, comprehensive theory completely explains them. Multiple explanations offer clues to how prejudice develops and survives — and how it can be defeated.

Humans are born without prejudiced beliefs, stereotyping thoughts and discriminating behaviors. These beliefs are taught, directly or indirectly, as we mature.

Children absorb the attitudes, beliefs, biases and prejudices of those around them. Since most learning occurs in a social context, the prejudices embedded in the culture are freely and easily transmitted. Children who grow up surrounded by patterns of prejudice simply conform to them. They mirror what they see.

Prejudice is an emotional learning that takes place early in life and persists as one gets older. Research on racial awareness suggests that children as young as preschool are aware of differences, including racial differences. This is developmentally appropriate and, by itself, not a problem. However, when negative emotions and values are attached to those differences, problems arise. As children mature they develop beliefs (stereotypes) that support their prejudices.

In adolescence young people experience a strong drive to be with other young people who have similar backgrounds, interests and values — to identify and bond with them. Having a sense of belonging — being part of a group — is essential to healthy development and self-esteem. The desire of children to associate with peers whose culture, religion and economic status is similar to their own is normal. However, this "birds of a feather flock together" drive can also rob children of the rich experience of diversity. As Daniel Goleman points out in his book *Emotional Intelligence* (Bantam, 1995), "The psychological price of loyalty to one's own group can be antipathy toward another, especially when there is a long history of enmity between the groups."

What Your School Can Do

Although schools cannot solve the problems of racial discord, they can do much to improve relations and reduce tensions and conflict among students of various races, abilities and ethnic backgrounds.

A good way to start is to ensure that your school's mission statement, norms, and policies support the value of diversity and contain sanctions for harassment in any form. These provide the foundation for a school climate that supports differences. Schools with healthy relations among diverse students don't shy away from the issue of diversity and differences. They look at these differences as enriching.

What You Can Do

A number of instructional and guidance strategies have been shown to decrease stereotyping, prejudice and discrimination. By incorporating these strategies wherever and whenever appropriate you will do much to promote tolerance among your students.

Maximize exposure to diversity. Students need to be exposed to lots of different people, opinions and viewpoints. They need to talk about who they are and get to know other children on a deeper level than classrooms and playgrounds normally permit. Research shows that the more students know about an ethnic group, the more tolerant they become. Genuine sharing and dialogue make it extremely difficult to view others as abstractions and stereotypes.

One of the primary tools in *Lessons in Tolerance and Diversity* is the Sharing Circle, a unique small-group discussion process that promotes personal sharing, openness, thoughtful discussion and acceptance. These values are embodied in many of the activities as well.

Promote teamwork and cooperative learning. Studies show that children playing and working together toward common goals develop positive attitudes about one another. Bands, choral groups, athletic teams, school clubs and community programs are examples of activities that can help to promote tolerance.

The same effect can be achieved in the classroom by having students work in heterogeneous cooperative learning groups. In small groups whose racial, ethnic and ability makeup is diverse, students learn *about* one another and *from* one another. In the process, they discover productive ways of working together. Reassigning students to new teams every few weeks encourages them to develop relationships with many children. Researchers have found a significant increase in the number of students who claim friendships with children of other races or ethnic groups after working together in cooperative teams.

The majority of the lessons in this book utilize some form of cooperative group interaction — team projects, joint problem solving, small- and large-group discussions, dramatizations, art projects and Sharing Circles, to name a few.

Provide opportunities for positive social interaction. Students need many opportunities to engage in a variety of positive interactions with other students. Social interaction activities not only develop understanding and appreciation, they boost the brain's ability to learn. In numerous books on learning and the human brain, Renate and Geoffrey Caine, (*Mindshifts : A Brain-Compatible Process for Professional Development and the Renewal of Education*, Zephyr Press, 1999) assert that academic achievement goes up when students feel included and cared about in class, are encouraged to care about others and are provided opportunities to work together in cooperative groups.

Research also indicates that students who get personally involved in the lesson are more likely to experience reduced prejudice. Activities that promote interpersonal interaction are among the most involving available to teachers and counselors. You will find abundant examples in this book.

Replace prejudiced thoughts. When students do express stereotyped or prejudiced beliefs — and they will — use thought replacement, not thought suppression, as an intervention device. Studies show that thoughts which are suppressed return with greater strength and possibly more resistance to being avoided in the future. Having people avoid thinking prejudiced thoughts either in structured exercises or informal ways is likely to create this rebound effect. Thought replacement is a more powerful and effective remedy. For example, a child who has a negative attitude about a classmate can be encouraged to find at least one specific likable quality or characteristic in the classmate. The child can then be coached to substitute the positive thought every time the negative thought occurs.

Thought replacement occurs naturally when students genuinely get to know each other in the safe and supportive environment of Sharing Circles. When children view each other as individuals stereotypes dissolve.

Develop critical thinking skills. According to recent studies, critical thinking may be the very best antidote to prejudice. Education that develops sophisticated cognitive skills — the ability to think critically and analytically — may produce more tolerant, less prejudiced individuals who are equipped to pass along their tolerance to the next generation.

Every lesson and Sharing Circle in this book concludes with discussion questions that encourage critical thinking. Many of the activities are designed to develop higher level cognitive skills as well.

How These Lessons Can Help

Lessons in Tolerance and Diversity is designed to counter influences that lead to fear and exclusion of others by helping students to develop self-awareness, esteem for self and others, communication and conflict management skills, and capacities for independent judgment, critical thinking and ethical reasoning.

The lessons are presented in a logical, developmental sequence, from valuing self and cultural identity through communication and conflict management to cooperation and team building.

Considerable attention is given to helping students understand and appreciate their own cultures and backgrounds. They must feel good about themselves in order to feel good about others.

Through the design of the activities and discussion questions, students share their ideas, beliefs and perspectives and interact with others who may or may not share their points of view. Out of this interaction they learn to withhold judgment, question their own ideas, exercise flexibility and, ultimately, embrace the richness of diversity.

How to Use the Lessons

Lessons in Tolerance and Diversity is divided into five instructional units:

1. **Celebrating Self and Cultural Diversity.** Students celebrate who they are, at the same time learning to appreciate others. They identify things they have in common as well as areas of difference.

2. **Getting Along: Communication and Conflict Management.** Students examine how differences lead to conflict and develop critical conflict management skills.

3. **Valuing Diversity in All Its Forms.** Color is just one difference that students distinguish and appreciate. Others include beliefs, practices, personal characteristics, values, family and cultural traditions.

4. **Shattering Stereotypes and Prejudice.** A variety of strategies are used to help students recognize the pervasive practice of stereotyping and to reject blind adherence to stereotypes in favor of reasoned thinking.

5. **Building A Caring Community: Team Building and Cooperation.** Activities help students recognize the benefits of cooperation and interdependence and the personal rewards that come from extending an embracing arm to others.

Lessons are arranged in a developmental sequence. While you are free to implement activities in any order you choose, for greatest impact we recommend adhering to the sequence provided.

Many of the activities are accompanied by *experience sheets*. Instructions for the use of these handouts are included in the activity directions. Experience sheets promote individual awareness and reflection and are never collected or graded, although students may be asked to discuss insights derived from experience sheets with their classmates.

At the conclusion of every activity is a list of discussion questions. Always allow enough time to facilitate a summary discussion; it is one of the most important parts of the activity. The questions are designed to stimulate critical thinking, ethical reasoning and dialogue. Furthermore, the benefits of an activity are maximized when students are given the opportunity to talk about the experience immediately afterwards, verbalizing their insights and making connections to events and conditions in their lives. Feel free to substitute questions that have greater relevance to issues the students are dealing with in the classroom, school or community. Do not use the summary discussion to sermonize or lecture or to force connections that the students are not ready to make. Do keep the questions open-ended (requiring more than a yes or no response) and use your best facilitation skills.

Lessons in Tolerance and Diversity contains close to twenty Sharing

Circles, powerful tools for promoting tolerance and celebrating diversity. Before leading your first circle, please read the section entitled "Extending the Learning: Sharing Circles."

Finally, please make appropriate adjustments for the ages, abilities and backgrounds of your students. We have included activities suited to a broad age range and are relying on you to do the fine tuning. As long as the spirit of each activity is preserved, we encourage all manner of reasonable adaptations. Diversity is good!

Checklist for Teachers and Counselors

As a counselor, teacher, or other educator, you can exert a powerful influence on the lives of the children with whom you work, helping them to develop tolerance for differences and an appreciation of diversity.

Use these guidelines when judging whether your teaching or counseling curriculum responds to and reflects the ethnic and cultural diversity of your students and of society:

1. Use books and materials that discuss and/or picture different races, ages, physical and learning abilities and economic levels, and that treat those differences honestly, realistically and sensitively.

2. Really get to know the students with whom you work. Accept each student as unique and special. Let students know that you recognize and appreciate their individual qualities. Children who feel good about themselves are less likely to be prejudiced against others.

3. Help students become sensitive to other people's feelings. Caring, empathic children are less likely to be prejudiced. In conflict situations, ask each student to think about how the other student is feeling.

4. When developing teaching/counseling goals and strategies, consider the different cultures and learning styles of the students. Then use your curriculum to strengthen each child's sense of identity.

5. Help children understand that there are similarities and differences within as well as among different groups. In many ways ethnic and racial groupings are arbitrary and misleading, implying relationships that may or may not exist.

6. Make sure that students understand that prejudice and discrimination are unfair. Make a firm rule that no person should be excluded or teased on the basis or race, religion, ethnicity, accent, gender, disability, sexual orientation or appearance. Point out and discuss discrimination when you see it.

7. Use your curriculum to acquaint students with persons of varying backgrounds and occupations within different racial/ethnic groups. In the classroom, provide opportunities for students to interact with many different students through project teams and cooperative learning groups.

8. Encourage students to take action on social problems they are concerned about and to point out prejudice and unfairness when they observe it.

9. Question and challenge students in ways that encourage critical thinking. For example, when a student makes a decision that reflects prejudiced thinking, ask her how that decision was reached and help her to reflect on and improve her decision-making process.

The highest result of education is tolerance.

Helen Keller

Celebrating Self and Cultural Diversity

Our Countries of Origin

Purpose:

To gain a deeper understanding of the diversity of students' backgrounds. The students will identify their countries of origin and demonstrate pride and self-esteem based on who they are and where they come from.

Materials:

writing materials for the students; U.S. and world maps; colored pins, flags or other map markers; whiteboard

Directions:

Introduce this activity by explaining that the United States is a land of many different people, all of whom have the right to share in its benefits and freedoms. Point out that no one ethnic group "owns" the U.S. because all of its citizens (other than Native Americans) or their ancestors came from some other land, and that many people represent a combination of backgrounds. Share with the students a bit about your own ethnic background and the lands from which your ancestors immigrated.

Next, tell the students they are going to do some individual research to find out what lands they, their parents, grandparents, or earlier ancestors came from. They will also learn some interesting things about the perceptions and experiences of these members of their family.

Have the students ask their parents and/or grandparents where they were born. Ask them to find out how and why their parents and/or grandparents came to the U.S. or to your part of the country from another region. Generate a list of questions for the students to answer by talking with family members or searching family records. (If you are working with very young children, send a note home explaining the activity and listing appropriate questions for the parents to answer.) Examples are:

- What kind of work did family members do in their country of origin?
- Where did they go to school and what was school like?
- Why did they come to the United States?
- In which U.S. states and communities have they lived?
- What was it like to leave home and go where they didn't know anyone or what to expect?
- What things were the same in both countries/regions and what things were different?
- What are some problems they encountered when they moved to the U.S.?

- Did family members experience any discrimination when the came to the U.S.? How have they handled it?
- What are some interesting facts or stories related to family origins or traditions?

Have the students report orally to the class. Schedule two or three reports each day and allow plenty of time for reactions and discussion. On U.S. and world maps, using colored pins or flags, mark the various places the students and their families/ancestors have lived. (For example, use one color to show countries of ancestral origin and a different color to mark places where the students have lived.)

Create a classroom chart listing every student along with his/her country or state of origin and ancestral countries of origin.

Discussion Questions:

1. *How many different countries are represented in our class?*
2. *Why is it important to take pride in and share our family and ethnic backgrounds?*
3. *What would school be like if all of us had exactly the same background and experience?*
4. *How does knowledge of our different ethnic backgrounds help promote cooperation and understanding?*

Extension:

Invite some of the parents/grandparents to visit the class and personally share their experiences.

An excellent follow up to this activity is the Sharing Circle, "Something I Like About Myself That Is Part of Me Because of My Culture," on page 91. (Be sure to read the section, "Sharing Circle Guidelines," on page 85.)

All humans, no matter how ethnically diverse, are essentially identical. We all are cut from the same cloth, made on the same patterns, granted the same strengths and weaknesses, and will ultimately share the same fate.

Shadow of Forgotten Ancestors

Carl Sagan and Ann Druyan

Diversity "R" Us

Purpose:

To provide an experience through which students develop awareness and appreciation of other cultures, and to encourage students to learn about each other's cultural and ethnic backgrounds.

Materials:

paper and writing implements, whiteboard, chart paper and markers

Directions:

Begin this activity by having the students think about what they learned from the student reports in the previous activity, "Countries of Origin." Ask, "Which countries and cultures that you heard about particularly interest you?" Facilitate sharing.

Next, pair students up so that, if possible, each student has a partner from a different country of origin. Explain that the pairs will interview each other to learn as much as they can about their partner's culture and country of origin. Next, brainstorm with the students questions they would like to ask their partners. List the questions on the whiteboard.

Possible questions are:
What foods are native to your country of origin?
What types of music are common there?
What particular crafts are created by people in this region or country?
How does a typical child/adult dress?
What customs are followed when a child is born, at birthdays and
*   weddings or when someone dies?*
What are some special holidays and how are they celebrated?
How do people define success?
Who are the heroes and heroines of this country or region?

Have the students choose 7 or 8 questions they would like to ask their partners. Tell them to write their chosen questions down leaving space between each one to record answers. Explain that, during the interview, if their partner can't answer one or more questions, they are to work as a team to research the answers. Set a due date for the completed interview reports.

As a way for each student to share something he or she learned from the assignment, create the following chart:

Student Name	Country of Origin	Something interesting we learned about the country or culture

Have each student report information learned about his/her partner's country of origin or region. Assign a recorder to add information to the chart as each report is given.

Discussion Questions:

1. *How can we all benefit from the various cultures represented in our class?*
2. *What do we gain by learning about the ethnic backgrounds of others?*

Extension:

Determine all the "native" languages of the students and have the students research and learn how to say a word or phrase in each language. Words or phrases such as "welcome," "please," "thank you," or "my name is _____," are good choices. Create a bulletin board display and have the students practice their words.

An excellent follow up to this activity is the Sharing Circle, "Something I Enjoy About Another Culture," on page 89.

The Chain of Diversity

Purpose:

To allow the students to describe something about their cultural heritage that they value, and to acknowledge valued aspects of cultural heritage in their classmates. To demonstrate understanding that strength exists in diversity.

Materials:

one copy of the Experience Sheet, "A Link in the Chain of Diversity" for each student, art supplies, scissors, and glue

Directions:

Ask the students to think about what they have been learning about their cultural background and the cultural backgrounds of their classmates. Ask them what the class would be like if everyone was just exactly alike. Invite them to share their ideas about how the class is enriched by the different backgrounds represented.

In your own words, explain that the strength and unity within a class can be compared to a chain with many individual links. Each culture is represented by a link that contributes to the common culture — the chain. If each link represents a different strength, uniting the links creates a chain that is longer and much stronger than any single link could ever be alone. Similarly, uniting gifts and talents found in a diverse classroom makes the group stronger by allowing every individual to benefit from the strength of every other individual. Ask the students to comment and to share their own ideas and insights.

Distribute the Experience Sheet, "A Link in the Chain of Diversity," and make sure the students understand the directions. When the students have finished creating their links, have them glue all the links together and display the Chain of Diversity in the room.

Discussion Questions:

1. *What have you learned from each other as a result of linking together your individual cultures?*
2. *Why is it important for us to respect and learn from the many cultures that contribute to our common culture?*
3. *Why is it important to show tolerance for the beliefs, practices and values of others?*

A Link in the Chain of Diversity
Experience Sheet

Things I value about my cultural heritage by _____

Cut out the link and decorate it with pictures and words that describe things you value about your cultural heritage. Draw and write on both sides. Make your link as creative and colorful as you can. Remember to write your name on the link, too. When you are finished, you and your classmates will glue your links together to form a long, strong, interesting chain.
Have fun!

Getting Along
Communication and Conflict Management

Developing Listening Skills

Purpose:

Students will learn and practice a process for "active listening" and develop an understanding of why effective listening is essential in helping people to understand each other and get along.

Materials:

one copy of the experience sheet, "5 Steps to Active Listening," for each student; whiteboard; several topics written on the board prior to the activity (see suggestions below)

Directions:

Tell the students that they are going to practice one of the most important communication skills they will ever learn — Active Listening. Write the term on the board, underline the word Active, and ask the students how they think active listening differs from the kind of listening they do all day long, every day.

Accept all ideas and begin to facilitate a discussion about the importance of listening. You might ask the students how they feel when someone really listens to them, and what it feels like to be interrupted or to realize that the other person didn't hear a word they said. In the course of your discussion, make the following points about listening:

- Good listeners are rare.
- In most conversations, people are more concerned with what they want to say than what the other person is saying.
- Good listening requires focus, concentration, and energy.
- To really listen, you have to keep an open mind and heart.
- Listening all by itself is the most effective way to help another person solve a problem or make a decision.
- People generally like to be around someone who is a good listener.

Distribute and review the "5 Steps to Active Listening" experience sheets. Discuss specific behaviors involved in each step, For example, point out that listening to the words requires thinking about and understanding their meaning *from the speaker's point of view.* Noticing feelings involves paying attention to the speaker's tone of voice, facial expression, and posture, and *empathizing* - imagining what it would be like to be in the speaker's shoes. Saying something back not only proves that you are listening, it helps the speaker clarify his/her thoughts and allows you to check to make sure you are "getting the message."

Demonstrate by asking a student to talk with you for a couple of minutes about something that is important to him/her. Instruct the students to watch carefully and notice what you do. Allow the demonstration to continue long enough for you to give four or five active listening responses. Then thank the volunteer and ask the observers to describe what they saw. Clarify the process and answer questions.

Have the students choose partners; then give the following directions:

Decide who is the speaker and who is the listener. Speakers, you will have 2 minutes to talk about a topic which I will announce. Listeners, you will demonstrate active listening behaviors. You will also listen carefully and try to remember everything that is said. When I call time after 2 minutes, listeners will have 1 minute to retell everything they remember hearing. Talk directly to the speaker and include any ideas, details, or specific language that you can remember. Finally, speakers will have 1 minute to correct anything that their listener misunderstood, as well as to describe how it felt to be listened to.

After the first round, have the partners switch roles and repeat the entire process using the same or a different topic. Allow 2 minutes for the speaker to address the topic, 1 minute for the listener to restate what she or he hears, and 1 minute for feedback to the listener by the speaker.

Suggested topics:
- My best school memory
- If I had a million dollars...
- If I ruled the world...

- My worst school memory
- If I were an animal...
- My favorite TV show or movie

Conclude the activity by discussing how it feels to be heard and understood. Explain that listening carefully to another person and *showing* that you are listening can be an effective way to resolve conflict, because what the other person may need most is to have his or her feelings and ideas listened to and accepted.

Discussion Questions:

1. *How did you feel when your partner showed that he or she was listening carefully to what you were saying?*
2. *Why do you think it is important to listen carefully to the other person and show that you are listening?*
3. *How can listening help resolve a conflict?*
4. *Why do people so seldom stop and really listen to each other?*
5. *How does active listening help people understand each other?*

Extension:

An excellent follow up to this activity is the Sharing Circle, "A Time I Listened Well," on page 94.

Five Steps to Active Listening
Experience Sheet

What is Active Listening? It's when you listen very carefully and try to understand the ideas and feelings of another person from his or her point of view.

Five Steps to Active Listening

1. Look at the person who is talking.
2. Listen carefully to his or her words.
3. Try to understand the meaning of the words.
4. Notice the feelings that go with the words.
5. Say something to show that you have been listening.

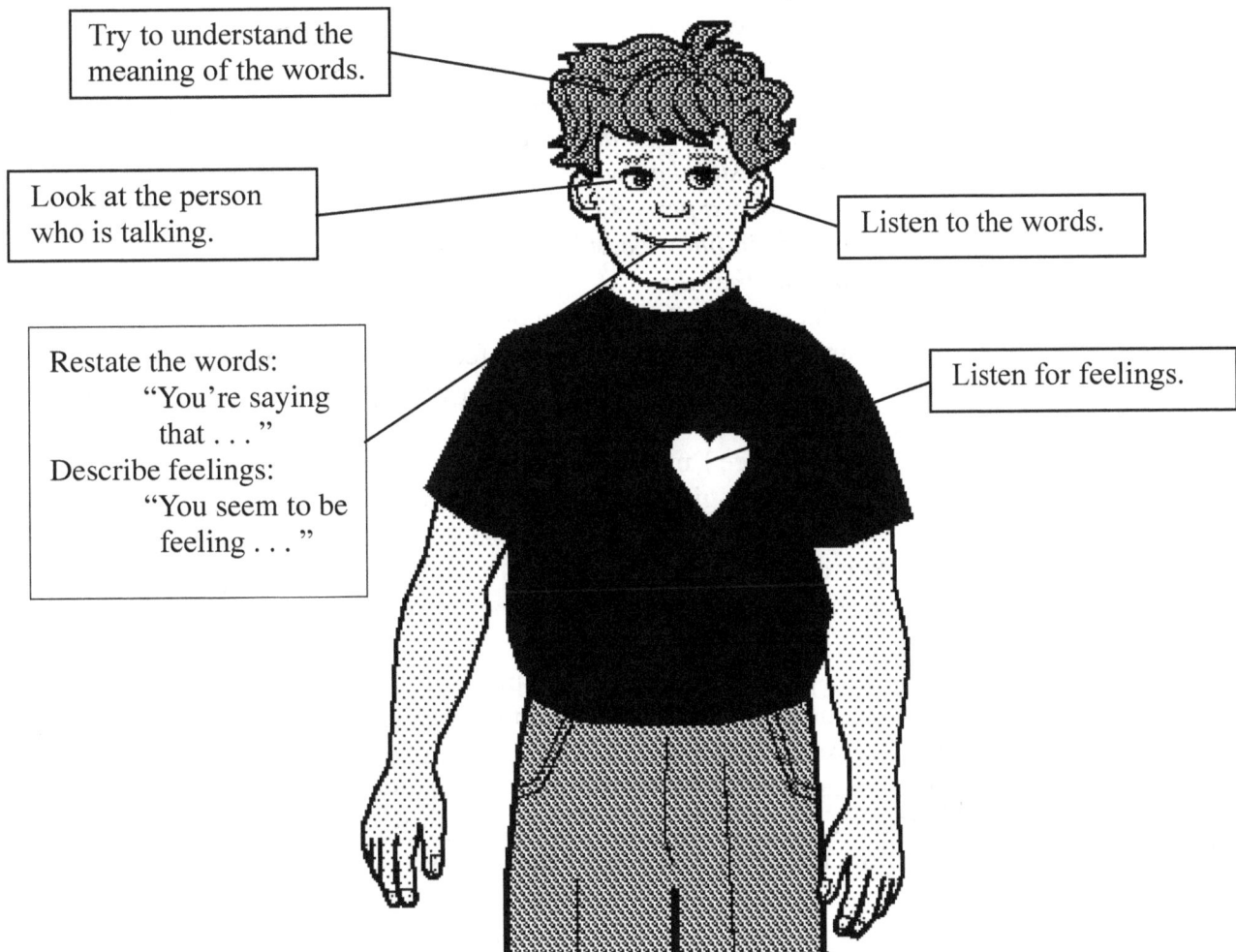

Try to understand the meaning of the words.

Look at the person who is talking.

Listen to the words.

Listen for feelings.

Restate the words:
"You're saying that . . ."
Describe feelings:
"You seem to be feeling . . ."

Put Downs and Destroyer Statements

Purpose:

This activity will help students develop an understanding of how negative statements can damage a person's feelings, ideas, and enthusiasm, as well as block communication. Students will also demonstrate alternative positive statements and describe methods of improving communication behaviors in themselves and others.

Materials:

whiteboard or chart paper

Directions:

Facilitate a discussion about appropriate and inappropriate ways to respond to another person's ideas, accomplishments, feelings, etc. In your own words, say:

Have you ever come up with a great idea that you couldn't wait to share with someone? But when you described your idea, the person you told made fun of it, or put you down in some way? Have you been afraid to share your strong feelings about something because you were certain no one would understand or, worse, you'd be ridiculed for your feelings? We can easily destroy a person's enthusiasm just by the things we say. We may not mean to do it, but we can kill their ideas and make them feel foolish for feeling the way they do.

Ask the students to help you brainstorm a list of statements that can hurt communication and damage the feelings, ideas, and enthusiasm of others. Write their ideas on the board or chart paper. Include statements such as:

Can't you see I'm busy?	What a stupid idea! Just like a guy.
Not bad for a girl.	That's a silly question.
Are you kidding me?	You shouldn't feel that way.
You can't be serious!	Don't be such a wimp.
Who asked for your opinion?	

Have pairs of volunteers role play some of the items from the list. Instruct one person to initiate an interaction and the other to respond using the "destroyer" statement. After each role play, invite the actors to describe their thoughts and feelings during the exchange. Then have the group think of at least three alternative positive responses that could be used in that situation. Role play and debrief those as well.

**Discussion
Questions:**

1. *Why do we respond to others with put downs and other types of destroyer statements?*
2. *Where do you think we learn this type of communication?*
3. *If you know someone who frequently makes these kinds of statements to you and others, what can you do about it?*
4. *How can you change your own bad communication habits?*

Extension:

Have the students observe and record all of the put downs and destroyer statements they hear at school, home, and play. Discuss their findings at the next session.

> *What diminishes one of us diminishes us all. But when a person is raised up, to that degree the world is lifted up.*
>
> *Mahatma Ghandi*

Conflict Words/Peaceful Words

Purpose:

In this activity students will be asked to write a conflict dialogue, mapping the escalation of the conflict from verbal sparring to physical violence and then to alter the dialogue to show how different words can change the direction of the conflict. They will also practice using calming vocabulary in stressful situations.

Materials:

chart paper and markers; writing materials for the students

Directions:

Before beginning this activity, conduct the Sharing Circle "I Got Into a Conflict," page 95. (Be sure to read the section "Sharing Circle Guidelines on page 85.) At the conclusion of the circle process, have the students form pairs. Tell them you want them to script the conflicts they just shared — to write a dialogue typical of each conflict situation.

Circulate and coach the students, helping them identify the words of the conflict and, through written dialogue, map the escalation of the conflict from verbal to physical fighting.

When the students have finished writing, ask them to help you develop a list of vocabulary associated with conflict. They should be able to take the words directly from their written dialogues. Record the words on chart paper so that the list can be saved. Expect statements like:

NO!

Shut up!

It's mine!

I had it first!

You nerd!

Stupid!

Note: When students want to express cussing or foul language in their scripts, have them do so with stars (***) and exclamation marks (!!!).

Next, turn the attention of the students to the language of peaceful conflict resolution. Have each pair take its first conflict dialogue and, at the point where the conflict is well established, begin to change the words, showing what must happen in order to end the conflict peacefully. When the pairs have finished with the first dialogue, have them rewrite the second one as well.

Chart the peaceful vocabulary in the same manner as the conflict vocabulary. Use the remaining time to role play some of the peaceful conflict resolution dialogues.

Note: Once the students understand the contrast between conflict vocabulary and resolution vocabulary and have scripted conflict dialogues, keep the focus on peaceful conflict resolution.

Variation:

At lower grade levels, develop the dialogue as a total group, with the students contributing ideas, and you recording.

Discussion Questions:

1. *Was it easy or hard to change your dialogue to include peaceful vocabulary? Why?*
2. *How hard do you think it is to change the type of words you're using in a real conflict situation? What do you think would make it easier?*
3. *How will this exercise help you resolve your own conflicts?*

Extension:

An excellent follow up to this activity is the Sharing Circle, "How I Handled a Disagreement with A Friend," on page 96.

We must not seek to defeat or humiliate an opponent, but to win friendship and understanding . . . Every word and deed must contribute to understanding.

Dr. Martin Luther King

What Do You See?

Purpose:

Through this creative experience, students will see that differences in perception and interpretation result in part from each person's uniqueness and that having different perceptions does not automatically make one person right and another wrong.

Materials:

one copy of the experience sheet, "What Do You See?" for each student; art materials

Directions:

Give each student a copy of the experience sheet, "What Do You See?". Ask the students to look at the lines for a few moments, allowing the lines to suggest a picture in their imagination.

Distribute the art materials. Direct the students to recall the picture in their imagination and draw it, incorporating the lines already on the page among the shapes and lines of their composition. Encourage independent work and discourage talking during this process. Assure the students that there is no right or wrong way to complete the assignment, but that you want each person to rely on his or her own creativity and imagination.

At the conclusion of the work period, go around the room and ask the students to share their pictures, describing how they perceived the preexisting lines and how they incorporated them in their compositions. Facilitate a follow-up discussion, emphasizing differences in perception and interpretation.

Discussion Questions:

1. Were any of our pictures "right" or "wrong?"
2. If we all saw the lines differently, what other things in life do you think we might see differently?
3. What things do we see or interpret differently that could cause problems and conflicts?
4. Why is it important to understand that people have a right to see and interpret things in their own ways?
5. What can happen when people believe that their perceptions are the right ones and different perceptions are wrong?

What Do You See?
Experience Sheet

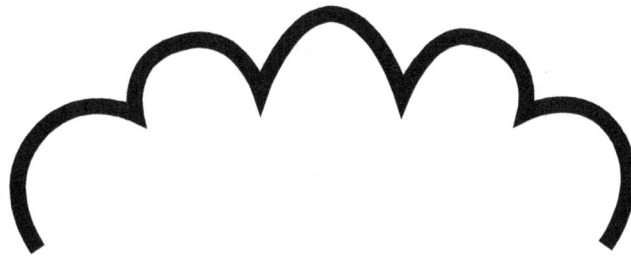

_____

Perceptions

Purpose:

This activity provides an opportunity for students to demonstrate how different perceptions often lead to conflict and to discuss ways of resolving conflicts caused by opposing views.

Materials:

one copy of the experience sheet, "Perceptions" for each student; whiteboard or chart paper and markers

Directions:

Write the word *perception* on the board, and ask the students to explain its meaning. Definitions might include:
- a mental image or picture
- a unique way of seeing and interpreting something based on past experiences

Point out that when two people see the same situation very differently — which happens often — the result can be disagreement, intolerance and conflict.

Distribute the experience sheets and go over the directions. Give the students a few minutes to complete the cartoons. Have them share their completed cartoons in groups of four or five. Conclude the activity with a total-group discussion.

Discussion Questions:

1. *What are people likely to do when their perceptions clash?*
2. *Is there always one right way of seeing something, and does that way make all other perceptions wrong? Explain.*
3. *What kinds of things might cause several of us to see the same incident quite differently?*
4. *What can you do to help two people resolve conflicting views?*

Extension:

An excellent follow up to this activity is the Sharing Circle, "How I Learned to Get Along With Someone Who Doesn't Think The Way I Do," on page 97.

Perceptions
Experience Sheet

Conflicts are often caused by differences in perception. Examine the following cartoons. Draw in the next frame for each cartoon, showing how differences in perception can lead to conflict.

Create a cartoon from your own experiences showing how conflict can arise from differences in perception.

Understanding the Other Point of View

Purpose:

The students will consider that every conflict situation has more than one point of view, and they will describe how understanding all points of view can help resolve conflicts.

Materials:

two pieces of drawing paper per student; colored markers, pencils or crayons; for the optional extension, one copy of the book, *Walk Two Moons,* by Sharon Creech (1994, Harper Collins)

Directions:

Say to the students, *When you are in a conflict, the other person's point of view, or perception, is often overshadowed by your own. Making an effort to understand the other point of view may help to resolve the conflict. An old Indian saying states that you can't judge another person until you have walked two moons (months) in his moccasins. In this activity, you will put yourself in the moccasins of another person and try to imagine his or her side of a conflict.*

Before having the students choose partners, give each person two pieces of drawing paper and some colored pencils, markers, or crayons. Provide these directions:

Draw the top view of a large pair of moccasins. Make the outline of the left moccasin on one sheet of paper and the right moccasin on the other sheet. Next, put a symbol or design in colors on the top forward part of each shoe. Use colored dots to represent beads and make your design stand for something about you. Finally, cut out both moccasins. Make the moccasins extra large so that they may be seen easily when placed on the floor.

When the moccasins are finished, ask the students to think of a conflict that they have had with another person, one in which they had a very clear point of view. Caution the students to choose a conflict that they are willing to share with a partner. Give the students time to think carefully about the conflict, writing it down on paper if necessary.

After each person has chosen a conflict, explain that in this activity the students will have a chance to look at that conflict from the other person's viewpoint, like "walking in another person's moccasins."

Have the students form dyads. Give these instructions:

Place your paper moccasins on the floor toe-to-toe with your partner's moccasins. Stand on your set of moccasins, facing your partner, and decide who is A and who is B. A's, you will tell your conflict story to your partner.

Express your point of view very clearly to your partner, including any personal feelings you have about the conflict. B's, your job is to suggest ways in which the story can be told from the other person's viewpoint. What would the other person in this conflict want? How would he or she feel?

Give the students time to carry out your directions. Then continue:

Now I want you to switch places with your partner. Stand on your partners moccasins. A's, retell your conflict experience, this time from the perspective of the other person. Recall the ideas your partner gave you and try to express the other person's thoughts, opinions, and feelings. B's, listen carefully. When your partner is finished telling the story from the other person's perspective, tell your partner how you think he or she did. Was your partner convincing? Did your partner really seem to be walking in the other person's moccasins?

Have the partners return to their own moccasins and repeat the activity with the B's acting as storytellers. When both partners have had a turn as conflict storyteller, ask several volunteers to share their stories with the whole group. Coach each volunteer to tell his/her story from both perspectives. Debrief the activity with a discussion concerning the importance of seeing the other person's point of view — particularly in a conflict.

Note: To ensure the success of this activity, you may need to demonstrate the dyad procedure with a volunteer.

Extension:

As a follow up to this activity, students may enjoy reading (or hearing you read) Sharon Creech's *Walk Two Moons*. In this story, Salamanca, a thirteen-year old girl, experiences many internal conflicts. When Salamanca's mother leaves her and her father; she promises to return but doesn't. At the end of the story, Sal and her grandfather play a game in which they take turns pretending to walk in someone else's moccasins. They talk about how they would feel and what they would do.

Discussion Questions:

1. *Was it easy or hard to "walk in the other person's moccasins" and tell the story from his or her point of view? Why?*
2. *Why is it important to think about a conflict from different points of view?*
3. *How can thinking about the other person's point of view help you avoid or resolve a conflict?*

I Have A Dream

Purpose:

Students will consider nonviolence as a positive action for conflict resolution and human good and that violence injures and destroys. This activity also explores the concept that all humans have worth and dignity regardless of their color, creed or social status.

Materials:

one copy of the "I Have A Dream" speech for each student; several of Dr. King's quotes (see next page) written on the whiteboard; writing materials for each student

Directions:

Begin this activity with a discussion of Dr. Martin Luther King, Jr., and his vision of justice and equality for all. Ask the students to share what they know about Dr. King and his leadership of the American civil rights movement. Point out that he believed in the basic goodness of people and in the philosophy of nonviolence. He had the courage to fight peacefully for the principles and values in which he believed. Refer to the selected quotes you have written on the board. Review one quote at a time and ask the students what they think Dr. King was saying. Remind the students that when Dr. King used the term "man" he was talking about *all* people — men and women of all ages and creeds.

Next, distribute copies of the "I Have A Dream" speech. Ask the students what they know about the circumstances under which this famous speech was delivered. Explain that on August 28, 1963, approximately 250,000 people from all parts of America — people of all races, ages and beliefs — went to Washington, D.C. to march from the Washington Monument to the Lincoln Memorial. The event was organized as the *People's March on Washington* for jobs and freedom and to show support for the proposed civil rights bill. For three hours the marchers and millions of television viewers listened to speeches delivered from the Lincoln Memorial. The speech most remembered is Dr. King's "I Have A Dream."

Read the speech as a group. Then ask the students what the speech means to them. Facilitate discussion, helping the students to grasp the vision of peace and equality reflected in the speech. Encourage discussion and thought by asking any or all of the discussion questions.

Culminate the discussion by asking the students to write their own versions of the speech. Emphasize that their speeches should focus on *their* dreams for the world and its peoples.

Allow time for the students to share and display their speeches in class.

Discussion Questions:

1. *What does Dr. King's vision of the world have to do with how we handle conflicts and differing views in our lives?*
2. *What has changed for minorities since the famous march on Washington? Do you think Dr. King's nonviolence approach has had an impact on those changes?*
3. *In what ways can we live our lives today that will honor Dr. King's beliefs?*
4. *What kind of world do you want to live in? What are you willing to do to make your vision a reality?*

Extension:

Have the students write editorials aimed at persuading people to take action against injustice.

Quotes from Dr. Martin Luther King:

"We must not seek to defeat or humiliate an opponent, but to win friendship and understanding . . . Every word and deed must contribute to an understanding."

"If we meet hate with hate, there will be more hate. From violence comes more violence."

"It is ultimately more honorable to walk the streets in dignity than to ride the bus in humiliation."

"The strong man is the man who can stand up for his rights and not hit back."

"Violence is immoral because it thrives on hatred rather than love. It destroys community and makes brotherhood impossible."

"The ultimate measure of a man is not where he stands in moments of comfort and convenience, but where he stands at times of challenge and controversy."

"Injustice anywhere is a threat to justice everywhere."

"We must all learn to live together as brothers and sisters or we will perish together as fools."

I Have A Dream

I have a dream that my four little children will one day live in a nation where they will not be judged by the color of their skin but by the content of their character.

I have a dream today.

I have a dream that one day the state of Alabama, whose governor's lips are presently dripping with the words of interposition and nullification, will be transformed into a situation where little black boys and black girls will be able to join hands with little white boys and white girls and walk together as sisters and brothers.

I have a dream today.

I have a dream that one day every valley shall be exalted, every hill and mountain shall be made low, the rough places will be made plain, and the crooked places will be made straight, and the glory of the Lord shall be revealed, and all flesh shall see it together.

This is our hope. This is the faith with which I return to the South. With this faith we will be able to hew out of the mountain of despair a stone of hope. With this faith we will be able to transform the jangling discords of our nation into a beautiful symphony of brotherhood. With this faith we will be able to work together, to pray together, to struggle together, to go to jail together, to stand up for freedom together, knowing that we will be free one day.

This will be the day when all of God's children will be able to sing with new meaning, "My country 'tis of thee, sweet land of liberty, of thee I sing. Land where my fathers died, land of the pilgrim's pride, from every mountainside, let freedom ring."

And if America is to be a great nation this must become true. So let freedom ring from the prodigious hilltops of New Hampshire! Let freedom ring from the mighty mountains of New York! Let freedom ring from the heightening Alleghenies of Pennsylvania!

Let freedom ring from the snow capped Rockies of Colorado!

Let freedom ring from the curvaceous peaks of California!

But not only that, let freedom ring from every hill and molehill of Mississippi. From every mountainside, let freedom ring.

When we let freedom ring, when we let it ring from every village and every hamlet, from every state and every city, we will be able to speed up that day when all of God's children, black men and white men, Jews and Gentiles, Protestants and Catholics, will be able to join hands and sing that old Negro spiritual,

"Free at last! Free at last! Thank God almighty, we are free at last!"

Delivered by Martin Luther King, Jr., March, 1963 at the Lincoln Memorial in Washington, D.C.

Valuing Diversity in All Its Forms

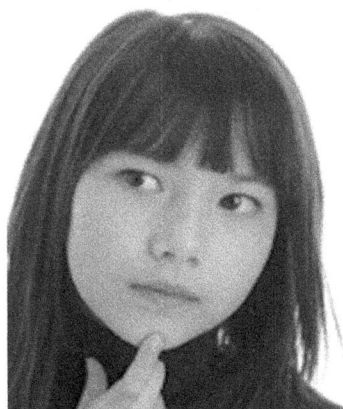

Unity Through Diversity

Purpose:

Through this activity, students will name specific ways in which people are different and the same and demonstrate that individual perception determines whether a characteristic is seen as a difference or a commonality. They will also recognize commonalities as vital to achieving understanding and harmony.

Materials:

whiteboard or chart paper

Directions:

Draw a horizontal line on the whiteboard, dividing a section of the board approximately in half. At the top of the board, write the heading, "Different." Begin the activity by asking the students to name all of the ways that human beings differ from one another. Write their suggestions below the heading and above the line. You will probably list such items as personality, preferences, skills, intelligence, traditions, culture, race, gender, abilities, physical appearance, socioeconomic status, etc. Keep going until the space above the line is crowded with items.

Write the heading, "Same," just below the line. Ask the students to name all of the ways in which humans are exactly the same. Suggestions will come more slowly this time. Be patient and see if someone comes up with the idea that all the items written above the line also represent ways in which people are exactly alike. (The idea is that all people possess personalities, skills, intelligence, etc., even though these attributes differ qualitatively from one person to another. In fact, this can be said for every item written above the line. All of these things not only make people different, they also make them the same.) If one of the students makes this observation, proceed from there. If no one discovers the concept, explain that you can add greatly to the list, and begin underlining items above the line, saying something like, "We all have different personalities, but we all have a personality," etc. Make the point that people are as much alike as they are different.

Explain that whether we see these items as differences or commonalities depends on our perception. When we focus only on the ways we differ, we tend to grow apart, but when we focus on commonalities, we tend to come together. This coming together creates strength in diversity. It can be thought of, too, as *unity through diversity* or *common ground.*

Tell the students that ALL successful teams are built on diversity. Using the example of personalities, demonstrate how everyone on a team has an individual personality, and that together those personalities make up the team personality. Members have different talents, skills, and knowledge to bring to a team. These differences are what make teams strong. Without diversity, a team cannot have much strength.

When individuals believe that their differences make them right or better (and make others wrong or worse) conflicts occur and prejudices develop. The need to see our differences as "right" or "wrong" destroys our ability to work together effectively. Encourage discussion by asking these and other questions.

Discussion Questions:

1. *What are some ways in which all people benefit from individual differences?*
2. *How can differences among group members contribute to their efforts when working on a joint endeavor?*
3. *How does the need to be "right" interfere with efforts to build on diversity?*
4. *Why do you think the world needs differences?*
5. *Why do we sometimes see differences as positive and at other times as negative?*
6. *How can we emphasize the positive aspects of diversity?*

Extension:

An excellent follow up to this activity is the Sharing Circle, "I Have A Friend Who Is Different From Me," on page 105.

We could all learn a lot from Crayons: Some are sharp, some are pretty, some are dull, some have weird names, and all are different colors... but they all have to learn to live in the same box.

Andy Rooney

Search for the One Person Team

Purpose:

This activity is designed to help students develop an awareness of the benefits and contributions of diversity to the makeup of groups and teams. The students will identify specific differences that contribute to a successful group endeavor.

Materials:

one copy of the experience sheet "Search for the One-Person Team," for each student

Directions:

Introduce the experience sheet by making the point that rarely is a successful endeavor accomplished by one person acting alone. Even when a single individual appears to have masterminded and carried out a project single-handedly, there are always other people in the background without whose cooperation and collaboration the finished product would not have been achieved.

Announce to the students that you want each of them to identify a group that is diverse and interdependent, and identify the different skills and talents that make the group successful. Explain that the students may choose any type of group they wish: a band, singing group, athletic team, club, business, etc. The group may be one to which they belong, or it may be a group they have observed in action or read about. A solo performer who works with a backup team or a support crew may also be considered a group.

Distribute the experience sheet, "Search for the One-Person Team." Announce that the students will have about 15 minutes to complete the sheet.

When the students have completed their experience sheets, ask volunteers to tell the class about the diverse makeup of the group they selected. After those students who wish to have shared, make the following points:

- No one can succeed in complete isolation.
- We all have gifts to contribute and those gifts are needed somewhere.
- Generally speaking, teams accomplish more than individuals accomplish.

Discussion Questions:

- When we choose to be *interdependent* with others, we are not becoming a *dependent* person, we are joining our resources with the resources of others in a common effort. Conclude the activity by facilitating further discussion.

1. *What is the difference between interdependence and dependence?*
2. *What kinds of diversity are essential for groups to be successful?*
3. *When you think about the group or team you selected, do you appraise the group by considering individual members or by considering the group as a whole? Why do you think that is?*
4. *Can you think of an individual who succeeded at something without the cooperation of others?*

Search for the One-Person Team
Experience Sheet

When people come together, they bring all of their unique personalities, viewpoints, talents, skills and ethnic diversity. When they apply these differences to achieving a common goal, wonderful things often happen. Take a moment to think of some groups and teams with which you are familiar. Pick a group or team that you think is successful because each member brings something unique and vital to the process.

Then complete the following:

Group Name:

What the group does:

Can you name the members of this group? List as many names as you can remember:

What talents and/or skills does each member of the group have?

What is the racial/ethnic makeup of this group?

What diverse physical characteristics can you identify among this group's members?

What makes this group stand out?

Disabilities: How Do They Feel?

Purpose:

To help students understand the challenges and frustrations of individuals who have disabilities. This activity also encourages students to look at people in their entirety, not just at their disability, and thereby to challenge stereotypes.

Materials:

blindfolds, cotton, shoelaces, mirrors (enough to correspond to the situations below); one index card for each student, with one of the following disabilities written on each card:

- What is it like to be blind? Wear a blindfold.
- What is it like to be deaf or hard of hearing? Stuff you ears with cotton.
- What is it like to have difficulty walking? Tie your legs together at the knees.
- What is it like to have difficulty talking when you speak? Keep your tongue on the roof of your mouth.
- What is it like to have difficulty getting your hands to do what you want? Use only your non-dominant hand.
- What is it like to have a learning disability? Do all your reading by looking at the words in a mirror.

Directions:

Write this list on the board and ask the students to prioritize how important these things are to them:
1. The ability to hear.
2. The ability to see
3. The ability to walk.
4. The ability to talk.
5. The ability to use heir hands
6. The ability to read and understand the written word.

Allow comments and discussion and then explain that they are going to have a chance to actually get an idea of what it's like to have some of these disabilities. Distribute the index cards, one per student, and explain that for the next hours (or longer if you think it is workable), they are to do everything with the disability they have been given on the index card. Pass out the blindfolds, cotton, shoelaces and mirrors to the appropriate students, and coach the students on how to proceed with their given "disability." You may need to provide helpers for the blindfolded students when they need to move around. Then proceed with your regular lesson. Allow enough time for the students to fully experience the difficulty of living with a disability. Going a full day, with the students exchanging disabilities half way through, will provide the most powerful lesson on disability awareness.

When all students have had a full experience of one or more of the disabilities, culminate with a class discussion.

Discussion Questions:

1. *How did you feel living with a disability?*
2. *Would learning be harder for you if you had to live with a disability all the time?*
3. *What methods did you develop to cope with your disability?*
4. *How did other people help you?*
5. *What kinds of special considerations would you have wanted to receive?*
6. *How did you feel about yourself?*
7. *Why do you think we did this activity?*
8. *What did you learn?*

What Do I Say?

Purpose:

This activity is designed to help students identify and demonstrate common mistakes in communicating with people who have disabilities and practice effective methods of communication.

Materials:

one copy of each of the five "Role Play Guidelines" on separate sheets of paper; whiteboard or chart paper and markers; props for the role plays (optional)

Directions:

Announce that the students are going to have an opportunity to contrast effective (and acceptable) and ineffective (and unacceptable) ways of communicating with people who have various disabilities.

On the whiteboard or chart paper, write these general guidelines and discuss them with the students:

- See the person who has a disability as a person, not as a disability.
- Don't talk down to the person. Avoid responding to persons with disabilities out of gratefulness for not having a disability yourself.
- Speak directly to the person who has a disability, not to a companion or an interpreter.
- Treat adults as adults. Don't use first names unless that familiarity is extended to everyone present.
- Be considerate. It might take extra time for the person with a disability to say or do things.
- Relax. Don't worry about using common expressions like, "See you later" or "I've got to be running along," when talking to persons with visual or physical disabilities.

Divide the class into five groups. Give each group a different sheet of "Role-Play Guidelines."

Explain that the groups are to read and discuss the communication guidelines for their category of disability, and then develop a two-part role play demonstrating:

1. Ineffective and/or unacceptable ways of communicating with a person who has that type of disability. These can be easily inferred from the guidelines and may be exaggerated for humor and effect.
2. Effective and acceptable ways of communicating with the same person.

Direct the groups to create whatever roles are necessary for the dramatizations they develop, including those of people with disabilities, friends, family, teachers, employers, health-care professionals, etc.

Allow the remainder of the class period for planning and rehearsing. At the next class meeting, have the groups take turns acting out their role plays, first demonstrating ineffective communication, then effective communication. Expect the ineffective methods to generate much laughter on the part of the audience. After each role play, ask audience members to describe as many of the guidelines as they can identify from watching the dramatization. Then have one of the actors read the entire list of guidelines to the class. At the conclusion of the role plays, post all of the guidelines on a bulletin board. Lead a follow-up discussion.

Discussion Questions:

1. *What did you learn as an actor in your role play that you didn't realize before?*
2. *What was particularly striking to you as an audience member?*
3. *What are some of the most common mistakes we make when communicating with people who have disabilities?*
4. *How do you feel now about your ability to communicate with people who have disabilities?*
5. *If you aren't sure how to communicate with a person who has a disability, what can you do?*

> *How beautiful a day can be*
> *when kindness touches it.*
>
> *George Elliston*

Role Play Guidelines

Communicating with Persons Who Have Speech Difficulties
1. Give your complete attention to the person who has difficulty speaking.
2. Be patient. Don't correct and don't speak for the person. Allow extra time. Give help when needed.
3. Keep your manner encouraging.
4. Ask questions that require short answers or a nod or shake of the head, when necessary.
5. If you have difficulty understanding, don't pretend. Repeat as much as you do understand. The person's reaction will clue you.

Communicating with Persons Who Have Hearing Loss
1. Get the person's attention. Wave your hand, tap the person's shoulder or bang on the table, if necessary.
2. Speak clearly and slowly. Don't shout or exaggerate lip movements. Keep sentences short.
3. Be flexible in your language. If the person has difficulty understanding you, rephrase your statement using simpler words. Don't keep repeating. If difficulty persists, write it down.
4. Provide a clear view of your face and keep the light source on it. Keep hands, food and other items away from your mouth when talking.
5. Be a lively speaker. Use facial expressions that match your tone of voice, and use gestures and body movements to aid communication.

Communicating with Persons Who Have Vision Loss
1. Introduce yourself and others who are with you. Use a normal tone of voice.
2. Use the person's name when starting conversation, so the person knows you are speaking to him or her. Let the person know when you are ending a conversation or moving away.
3. Ask the person if he or she wants help. When giving assistance, allow the person to take your arm, which helps you to guide. Warn the person of any steps or changes in level. Use specifics such as *left* and *right.*
4. Offer seating by placing the person's hand on the back or arm of the seat.
5. Don't pet a guide dog. Remember to walk on the side of the person away from the dog.

Communicating with Persons Who Use Wheelchairs or Crutches

1. Don't lean or hang on a person's wheelchair. It is part of that person's body space.
2. Sit, squat, or kneel if conversation continues for more than a few minutes. Don't be a "pain in the neck."
3. Ask a wheelchair occupant if he or she wants to be pushed *before* you do so.
4. Allow a person who uses a wheelchair or crutches to keep them within reach. Many wheelchair users can transfer to chairs, car seats, etc. Some wheelchair users can walk with crutches part of the time.
5. Consider distance, weather conditions, and surfaces such as stairs, curbs, or inclines when giving directions.

Communicating with Persons Who Have Mental Retardation

1. Speak slowly and distinctly. *Show* might be more effective then *tell*.
2. Tell the person what to do, not what *not* to do.
3. Help the person feel comfortable. Maintain nonthreatening voice and facial expressions.
4. Treat the adult person who has mental retardation as an adult.
5. Base exceptions to rules on reason, not pity.

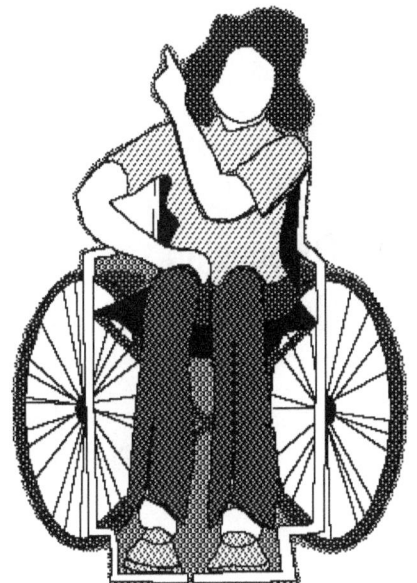

It's An Interdependent World

Purpose:

    In this activity students investigate the contributions of people with disabilities, both contemporary and historical, and people of diverse ethnic and racial backgrounds. By appreciating the contributions of this diverse group, students will develop respect and understanding.

Materials:

    whiteboard; writing materials for the students

Directions:

    Brainstorm with the students a list of famous people, both contemporary and historical, who have made a contribution to society. Have the students name as many as they can think of that have a disability and/or represent diverse cultural backgrounds. As names are suggested, list them on the board. When a good list has been created, have each student choose one person to research. Have the students share what they have learned by giving oral reports or presenting short skits to the class. If they choose skits, have them work in small groups to prepare and present.

Suggested names to research

    Mary McLeod Bethune, African-American educator • Chief Joseph, leader of the Nez Perce Indians • Martin Luther King, Jr., civil rights leader • Severo Ochoa, Spanish-American biochemist • Ludwig Von Beethoven, deaf German composer • Louis Braille, blind French inventor of the Braille system • Barbara Jordan, African-American congresswoman with Multiple Sclerosis • Franklin D. Roosevelt, U.S. President with polio • Alex Haley, African-American author • Cesar Chavez, Mexican-American farm worker • Minoru Yamasaki, Japanese-American architect • Sacajawea, Shoshone Indian guide to Lewis and Clark • Whoopi Goldberg, African-American learning disabled actress • Harriet Tubman, African-American leader of the underground railroad • Rosa Parks, African-American civil rights activist • Barack Obama, first African-American U.S. President • Madame C. J. Walker, daughter of former slaves and the first African-American woman millionaire • Sonia Sotomayor, first Latina Supreme Court justice.

Discussion Questions:

1. *What have you learned about the abilities of human beings to improve life for themselves and others?*
2. *Why is it important to learn about the contributions of different people?*

Shattering Stereotypes and Prejudice

How Would You Feel?

Purpose:

Through this activity, students will examine racial/cultural issues and related feelings.

Materials:

one copy of the experience sheet, "Put Yourself in This Situation," and writing materials for each student

Directions:

Distribute the experience sheets. Give the students time to answer each question on their separate sheets of paper. If you want to encourage longer, more thoughtful responses, ask the students to complete them as a homework assignment.

Note: Allow the students to approach the questions in any way they choose. Some of the questions are worded so that they may represent the view of either a minority or a majority person. This ambiguity could add interest to the discussion.

Ask the students which question they want to discuss first. Give students who are particularly troubled or confused by an item the opportunity to air their concerns. Encourage the sharing of personal experiences similar to those described.

If your group is large, have the students share in dyads before convening a group discussion. As each item is discussed, ask the questions listed below along with other relevant open-ended questions.

Discussion Questions:

1. *What is really going on in this situation?*
2. *What would your very first feelings be in this situation? What about later?*
3. *What do you think you would say or do in this situation?*
4. *What, if anything, would you like to see done about this kind of situation? What are you willing to do?*

Extension:

An excellent follow up to this activity is the Sharing Circle, "I Was Labeled Based On Something I Couldn't Change," on page 102.

Put Yourself in This Situation
Experience Sheet

On a separate piece of paper describe how you would feel in each of these situations:

How would you feel if...

1. You had to pay "up front" before being served at a restaurant?

2. The fences and walls in your once nice neighborhood were being covered with graffiti?

3. You'd been waiting in a long line and when it was your turn, the clerk ignored you and went on to the next person?

4. Women visibly clutched their handbags tighter when you passed them on the street?

5. You couldn't get into the college you wanted because the rest of the openings were reserved for minorities?

6. You were stopped for no apparent reason other than your appearance and asked to prove your legal residency?

7. Your little brother/sister didn't understand the social slights and racial slurs of other kids, and you had to explain them to him/her?

8. Your parents wouldn't let you date a person you really liked because of his/her race?

9. People were always getting impatient — even angry — with you because of your heavy accent in English?

10. You kept getting passed over for promotions, which went to workers less qualified than you?

11. You were never invited when your friends went swimming at a private club?

12. Your parent gently suggested that you spend less time with your friend of a different race?

What Is Tolerance?

Purpose:

In this activity students will examine the issue of tolerance in the context of a current event. They will also identify common acts of intolerance between individuals and groups and describe ways of demonstrating greater tolerance for themselves.

Materials:

a short news article about an incident relating to tolerance/intolerance between individuals or groups

Directions:

Begin by reading the news article to the group. If the group is small, pass the article around and allow the students to examine it individually or in pairs. Then ask the group one or more of these questions:
— *What is tolerance?*
— *What does it mean to be tolerant of another person or group?*
— *Who was tolerant /intolerant in this article?*
— *Toward whom was the tolerance/intolerance directed?*
— *What caused the tolerance/intolerance?*
— *What effects did the tolerance/intolerance have?*

Ask the group to brainstorm ways in which different groups show intolerance toward each other. For example:
• different racial/ethnic groups • boys and girls • women and men • different religions • democrats and republicans • straight people and gay people • neighbors • pet owners and non-owners • adults who have children and childless adults • thin people and fat people

Examples: Women shouldn't be fire fighters, run for President, or serve in combat units; people don't like to see men cry; an earring means a man is gay; boys are teased for playing with dolls; people of different races who marry are scorned; black people have a harder time finding jobs; etc.

Lead a culminating discussion focusing on specific things that the students and others can do to increase tolerance.

Discussion Questions:

1. How can people of different races become more tolerant of each other? What about religions?

2. What can you do to help ease neighborhood intolerance of two big dogs that are friendly, but sometimes bark or mess on other people's lawns?

3. What can you do if some of your friends are saying intolerant things about another kid who is fat? ... dresses differently because of his/her religion or culture? ... has a disability?

4. What can you do to show your tolerance of people and groups that are different from you?

Extension:

An excellent follow up to this activity is the Sharing Circle, "A Way I Show Tolerance," on page 99.

The world is too dangerous to live in—not because of the people who do evil, but because of the people who stand by and let them.

Albert Einstein

Shattering Stereotypes

Purpose:

This activity is designed to help students better understand the nature of prejudice and stereotyping and to develop strategies for being tolerant of differences.

Materials:

one copy of the "Shattering Stereotypes" experience sheet for each student

Directions:

Ask the students if they know what *stereotype* means? What *prejudice* means? Come up with a class understanding of both words. Use the dictionary if necessary. Write the agreed upon definitions on the board. Point out that prejudice often begins with a bad experience that is generalized into a stereotype. Explain this concept by having the students think of a person who is different from themselves with whom they had a bad experience. The difference doesn't need to be ethnic or racial and the person could be anyone — a dentist, doctor, police officer, teacher, big kid, etc. Ask volunteers to share some of their experiences. As they share, ask, "Did your bad experience develop into a prejudice? Why or why not?" Next distribute the experience sheet, "Shattering Stereotypes." Ask the students to complete each line with the first thing that comes to mind. Ask them not to stop and think but just to write their responses. Point out that stereotypes are not always negative — they can sometimes be positive. Give the students a couple of minutes to complete the first part of the experience sheet, then ask them to share some of their responses. Encourage discussion by asking these and other questions:
  • Where do you think you learned the stereotyped ideas you wrote down?
  • Which stereotypes bother you most?
  • How do stereotypes perpetuate prejudice?
  • What can we do to eliminate stereotypes?
Ask the students to complete their experience sheets and to keep them handy because they will be using them for another activity.

Extension:

For one week, have the students look through newspapers and magazines, look online, read ads, listen to music, and watch TV and videos while on the lookout for stereotyping or prejudicial remarks. Ask them to keep a list of what they find and to report back to the class.

Shattering Stereotypes
Experience Sheet

Write down your first reaction to each statement.
Don't take time to think about it — just write.

   Indians all/always

   Mexicans all/always

   Football players all/always

   Blonds all/always

   Texans all/always

   Skinheads all/always

   Blacks all/always

   Italians all/always

   Arabs all/always

   Teachers all/always

   Teens all/always

   Boys all/always

   Girls all/always

   Old people all/always

   Police all/always

   Asians all/always

   Whites all/always

   Americans all/always

   Hollywood stars all/always

   Millionaires all/always

   Politicians all/always

Identify at least one person for each category who doesn't fit the stereotype. It can be someone you know or a famous person. Write his or her name in the blank space on the left side.

Remember this: Whenever you catch yourself thinking a prejudiced or stereotypical thought about a group or individual, stop and think of three exceptions to the prejudice or stereotype.

Looking at Positive Attributes in Others

Purpose:

The students are asked to focus on the positive attributes and strengths of others, they will acknowledge their own attitudes, feelings and beliefs toward those who appear to be different. This can be a beginning to breaking down some barriers between students and the development of tolerant attitudes.

Materials:

the experience sheets, "Shattering Stereotypes" from the previous activity; writing materials for each group

Directions:

Divide the class into small groups of 4 or 5. Ask the students to refer to their "Shattering Stereotypes" experience sheets. Instruct each group to pick one category from the list, making sure that there are no duplications. Next, have each group brainstorm all the positive attributes they can think of for their particular population of people and to write down all their ideas. Circulate and offer assistance, as needed, allowing enough time for the creation of ample lists.

Note: Caution the students to avoid listing more stereotypes (*e.g.,* "Blondes are fun," "Texans give great barbecues," "Blacks are athletic"). To steer clear of this trap, suggest that they think of specific people they know in each category and list qualities they've admired in those people.

Once the lists have been completed, ask each group to demonstrate as many of the positive attributes as they can to the rest of the class. Tell them they can do this in any way they choose — with a skit, a story, a picture, etc. Whatever creative way they design will be fine. Set a time for the presentations and encourage a positive, enjoyable, affirming experience for all.

Discussion Questions:

1. *Which is easier to look at, positive qualities of people who are different from you, or negative qualities? Why?*
2. *Why is it important to look at people as individuals rather than as members of a group?*
3. *Are you likely to become friends with someone if you only focus on what you see as that person's negative qualities? What do you need to focus on?*
4. *When were you completely wrong about another person because of a prejudice or stereotype?*
5. *How can we deal with people who tease others by using ethnic humor or slurs?*

Ways to Fight Prejudice, Stereotyping and Discrimination

Purpose:

To develop in students an awareness that "turning a blind eye" or standing by and doing nothing to prevent acts of racism, discrimination and stereotyping allows, in the words of Daniel Goleman, "the virus of prejudice to spread unopposed." This activity encourages students to develop guidelines for noticing, speak up and taking a stand against acts of prejudice.

Materials:

whiteboard; writing materials for the students; marking pens and several large sheets of poster paper or poster board for the final chart

Directions:

In your own words, say to the students:

Racism is a serious problem in many schools today. Our school is no exception. At times you may have witnessed name-calling, slurs, threats and even fights. In some schools racial hate groups like the "skinheads" spend their time harassing and terrorizing minority students.

Racism hurts everyone. It promotes stereotypes and prevents people from really getting to know each other. It can have a terrible effect on a person's self-worth and self-esteem.

What are some acts of racism, prejudice or discrimination that you have witnessed here at school or elsewhere? (Facilitate discussion, cautioning students not to identify the people involved by name).

What could have prevented these incidents from occurring?

As a total group, brainstorm some of the factors involved in overt and covert racism and intolerance. Write all ideas on the board or chart paper. The students will need this list later while working in small groups. Try to elicit these and other ideas:

- Instead of objecting to racist remarks, people often ignore them. Some students snicker or laugh at racist jokes instead of saying "That's not funny."
- Acts of discrimination and favoritism (for example, when most awards or elected offices go to students of one race) often go unnoticed and unchallenged. Vigilance and activism are needed to stem such practices.
- Kids tend to hang out with other kids who are like them, racially as well as in other ways. Reaching out to and befriending students from other groups promotes understanding and is personally rewarding.

- People are quick to label normal conflicts between individuals as "racially motivated" when in fact they are no different from conflicts between people of the same race. This retards communication and makes it difficult to resolve differences productively.
- People are afraid to talk about their racist feelings. We all have prejudices. Instead of pretending we don't or ignoring them, we need to get them out in the open and discuss them.

Have the students form small groups of 6 to 8 using the group list just created as a springboard. Tell them that you want each group to brainstorm strategies that the entire student body can use to promote tolerance and diversity. Have each group appoint a recorder to write down all ideas. Suggest that each strategy begin with an "action word" that says what the individual student must do to carry out that strategy. Examples of action words are: *work, reach out, stand up, promote, accept, speak up, learn, talk to, join.*

Allow at least 15 minutes for brainstorming. Circulate and offer encouragement as needed. Then have each group read its ideas to the rest of the class. Using the discussion questions below, facilitate discussion.

Have a team of two or three volunteers compile all of the strategies into a single list, combining similar items. Then, at a later session, work with the class to reduce the list to no more than 10 strategies. Be sure each of the final strategies is worded clearly and includes examples of specific behaviors. Have the same (or a different) team of volunteers make the final chart or poster. Display it in the classroom and elsewhere in the school.

Discussion Questions:

1. *Why is it important to fight racism actively and openly?*
2. *Why do so many people ignore racist remarks, jokes and behaviors?*
3. *What impression does a racist person get when his or her remarks and actions are tolerated by others?*
4. *What can you do to help promote tolerance and diversity?*

Extension:

An excellent follow up to this activity is the Sharing Circle, "Something I Respect About A Person of A Different Race or Culture," on page 92.

How Does Prejudice Feel?

Purpose:

    This activity allows students to feel what it is like to be discriminated against because of a superficial characteristic. In the process the students define the terms *prejudice*, *stereotype* and *discrimination*, gradually drawing understanding from the immediate experience of the activity. The students then listen to the story of teacher Jane Elliott who conducted a similar experiment with her students following the assassination of Martin Luther King, Jr. In a follow-up discussion, they relate their experience to discrimination in society at large.

Materials:

    non-permanent marking pens in two colors; whiteboard; writing materials for the students

Directions:

    As the students enter the room, mark their left palm with either an X or an O. Instruct the students at the beginning of class to show the marked palm whenever they raise their hands to ask a question. Do not offer any further explanation for the marked palms.
    Write the following words on the whiteboard:
        Prejudice
        Stereotype
        Discrimination

    Ask the students to help you define the meaning of each word. However, as the students raise their hands to suggest ideas, call on only the X's. Facilitate the discussion and the formulation of each definition just as you would normally, while ignoring the O's and lavishing praise and positive reinforcement on the X's. Say things like:
        That's an excellent insight, Mike.
        Yes, yes, Monica, you are absolutely correct.
        You X's are really sharp today.

    Within a very short time, the O's will stop raising their hands, become distracted, and find other things to occupy their attention. Some will realize what you are doing, but others will not. As soon as you have "lost" almost all of the O's, finish defining whatever word you are on and then stop. Ask the students:
        What's been happening here?

Invite the students to give their reactions to the process. When accused of favoring the X's, admit it. Then quickly proceed to the next stage of the experiment. Have every X pair up with an O. In your own words, say to the students:

> Actually, I knew all along that the O's were the smartest group and would have the best ideas. I just wanted to give the X's a head start because I knew they needed it. But since the X's didn't get very far, it's time they got some help from the O's. Your assignment is to work with your partner to define the rest of the words. Use the dictionary if you like, and write down your own ideas. O's, you will have to take the lead, because the X's need some help. X's, pay attention to the O's.

Have the pairs proceed with the assignment. Allow this part of the experiment to continue for several minutes. You will probably notice that the O's, rather than show empathy based on their earlier experience, will take great pleasure in dominating the X's. When you think the X's have had ample time to experience their share of discrimination, stop the activity. Say to the students:

> What I just did is very much like what another teacher did over forty years ago. Listen while I tell you her story.

The day after Martin Luther Kind was assassinated, Jane Elliott, a third-grade teacher, decided that she wanted her students to really understand what it felt like to be discriminated against.. These students had heard a great deal about prejudice, but none of them had ever experienced it. They lived in a small town in Iowa. Most of the people in their town looked pretty much alike, had the same background and seemed to share most of the same values and goals. The teacher wanted to create a situation in which the students would experience the effects of prejudice. She decided to use eye color as the basis for discrimination. People had for years been treated unfairly because of their skin color, type of hair and religion, so why not use eye color? The students agreed, and so they were separated into a blue-eyed group and a brown-eyed group.

Since the teacher was blue-eyed, she decided that on the first day of the experiment the blue-eyed students would be "better" and on the next day they would change roles and the brown-eyed students would be "better." This way both groups had the chance to experience what it felt like to be "superior" and "inferior."

At first the class felt that the game would be fun. They laughed together and looked forward to the first day of the experiment. All that changed when:

- *The blue-eyed students were allowed to sit in the front of the room, while the brown-eyed students were forced to sit in the back.*
- *The brown-eyed students had to wear collars around their necks for identification.*
- *The teacher made fun of the brown-eyed students when they didn't know the right answers.*
- *At recess, only the blue-eyed students were allowed to use the playground. The brown-eyed students had to stay inside.*
- *At lunch the blue-eyed students were allowed to go to the head of the line and take extra servings, while the brown-eyed students had to wait and only got one serving.*

It wasn't long before the blue-eyed students started making fun of the brown-eyed students, calling them "brownies," lazy, stupid and dirty. Angry and hurt, the brown-eyed students began resisting, which led to fist fights and shoving matches. Then the brown-eyes students started falling behind in class. They became "dumb" because they were being treated like dummies. While the blue-eyed students were happy to be receiving extra attention and enjoyed feeling "superior," the brown-eyed students felt resentful and left out and eventually gave up and just went along with the situation.

On the second day of the experiment, the roles were switched and the brown-eyed students became "superior" to the blue-eyed students. The same thing happened. Students who had always been cooperative and well-mannered suddenly changed and became mean little bullies. The experiment proved that all people are capable of prejudiced behavior and it frightened the teacher very much. For more than twenty years after that first experience, Jane Elliott duplicated her experiment with adults in all walks of life in her effort to fight racism.

Tell the students that you wanted them to experience prejudice, stereotyping and discrimination in just the same way that the students in the story experienced it — first hand.

Use the discussion questions to facilitate a discussion about the entire experience. In the course of the discussion, finish defining the terms.

Discussion Questions:

1. *How did you feel when you were part of the "inferior" group?*
2. *What was it like to hear the other group getting all that praise and attention when you knew that your ideas were just as good?*
3. *How did you feel when I implied later that your group wasn't very smart?*
4. *On what basis was I discriminating against each group?*
5. *Were there any good reasons for me to favor the X's? ...the O's?*
6. *What groups in our country have been, or are, stereotyped based on something superficial like eye color or an X or O?*
7. *What if this were not just a short lesson? How would you feel if you were treated every day like you were slower or less capable? How would you act? How well would you do in school?*
8. *How is it different to judge a person by the color of his/her skin or by his/her religion than by the color of his/her eyes?*

For Further Information

The activity outlined here is a greatly shortened version of the original exercise conducted by Jane Elliott. Several documentaries have been made of the original experiment as well as of Jane Elliott's continued work conducting this experience around the world with many different populations. There is much material available on the internet including videos and lesson plans. For information go to
www.pbs.org/wgbh/pages/frontline/shows/divided

As long as you keep a person down, some part of you has to be down there to hold him down. So it means you cannot soar as you otherwise might.

Marian Anderson

Using Literature for Teaching Tolerance

Purpose:

Short stories and novels are an excellent way to help students explore the lives of people whose cultures are different from theirs, to learn about problems created by stereotyping people, and to empathize with the feelings experienced by victims of stereotyping.

Materials:

examples from literature that deal with problems related to stereotyping and/or cultural differences; unlined paper and pencils or markers

Directions:

Begin this activity by discussing the meaning of the word *stereotype*. If you have done this in a previous activity, refer to the earlier definition. Ask if any students know what it means to stereotype another person, or if they can give an example of stereotyping. If necessary, give the students a definition and provide examples yourself. In your own words, explain:

To stereotype means to have a fixed idea about a particular group of people and to judge all members of the group according to that idea. Stereotyping means making assumptions about people based on little knowledge. For example, some people think that girls are afraid of bugs and snakes. They don't look at the individual girl and decide whether or not she is afraid. Other people think that boys can't play with dolls because dolls are for girls. They don't consider that a boy might be pretending to be "Daddy" while holding a doll. Another example involves ideas some individuals have about rich people and poor people. They think that all rich people are snobs and all poor people are lazy. These assumptions stereotype people. Stereotyping leads to prejudice, which involves judging people or treating them badly because of a belief about them that is usually wrong to begin with.

Share with the students incidents of stereotyping and prejudice that have occurred in your life or the life of someone you know. Think of examples related to academic ability (nerd or dummy), gender (stupid girl or awkward boy), athletic ability (jock or klutz), color of hair (dumb blonde), race (stupid, lazy, greedy, cheap), economic status (poor white trash), or religion (ugly names given to members of a religious group). Ask the students how they would feel if someone said something untrue about them because of stereotyping.

Read aloud a story from literature in which stereotyping takes place. A suggested list appears at the end of this activity. When you complete any portion of the story in which a character is stereotyped, stop reading and distribute unlined paper. In your own words, explain:

This activity is called "Open Mind." I want you to draw pictures and words to show what you think is going on inside the mind of one of the book characters. First, draw a large outline of a head on your paper. Choose one character from the passage I just read in the book. Write the name of that character on the bottom of the paper, under the outline of the head. Next, imagine what that character is thinking and feeling during these moments in the story. Inside the outline of the head, draw pictures and symbols and write words to represent the character's thoughts. Put as many pictures, symbols, and words as you like inside the "Open Mind," as long as they represent what you think your chosen character is thinking and feeling.

When everyone is finished, invite the students to share their "Open Minds," explaining the meaning of the pictures, symbols and words. If time permits, repeat the entire process using a new passage from the same story, or from a different story. Conclude the activity by asking questions to stimulate discussion.

Discussion Questions:

1. What would you like others to know and understand about you?
2. How can we help prevent people from stereotyping us and others?
3. What are some of the consequences of stereotyping?
4. How does the stereotyper lose by refusing to see people as individuals?

Literature List:

Grades K-3
Amazing Grace, by Mary Hoffman 1991
Angel Child, Dragon Child, by Michele Surat 1989
The Hundred Dresses, by Eleanor Estes 1944
Clive Eats Alligators, by Alison Lester 1986
How My Parents Learned to Eat, by Ina Friedman 1984
Oliver Button Is A Sissy, by Tomi de Paola 1979
Frederick, by Leo Lionni 1967
Here Comes the Cat, by Frank Asch and Vladimir Vagin 1970
All The Animals, by William Wondriska 1970
William's Doll, by Charlotte Zolotow

Grades 4-8
So Far From The Sea, by Eve Bunting 1989
The Skin I'm In, by Sharon G. Flake 1998

Gypsy Rizka, by Lloyd Alexander 1999
Amistad, A Long Road to Freedom, by Walter Dean Myers 1998
Maniac McGee, by Jerry Spinelli 1991
Teammates, by Peter Golenbock 1990
No Pretty Pictures: A Child of War, by Anita Lobel 1998
Beyond the Mango Tree, by Amy Bronwen 1998

Young Adults
Yoruba Girl Dancing, Simi Bedford 1994
The Ceremony of Innocence, by Jamake Highwater 1985
Saying Goodbye, by Marie Lee 1994
The Sunita Experiment, by Mitali Perkins 1993
Hold Fast to Dreams, by Andrea Davis Pinckney 1995
Silent Words, by Ruby Slipperjack 1992
My Name Is Seepeetza, by Shirley Sterling 1992
Fast Talk on a Slow Track, by Rita Willimas-Garcia 1991
Thief of Hearts, by Laurence Yep 1995
Annie John, by Jamaica Kincaid 1983
Kitchen, by Banana Yoshimoto 1988
My Son's Story, by Nadine Godimer 1990
How the Garcia Girls Lost Their Accents, by Julia Alvarez 1991
The Giver, by Lois Lowry 1993
Breath, Eyes, Memory, by Edwidge Danticat 1994
Girl, Interrupted, by Susanna Kaysen 1994

> *The Holocaust did not begin with the building of crematoria, and Hitler did not come to power with tanks and guns; it all began with uttering evil words, with defamation, with language and propaganda.*
>
> *Rabbi Abraham Joshua Heschel*

Stereotypes in the Movies

Purpose:

The fondness that most young people have for movies can be used with great advantage to help students recognize and analyze the forces that influence stereotyping and to be aware of the myths surrounding stereotypes.

Materials:

any movie dealing with any stereotype (see suggested list)

Directions:

The fondness that children and teens have for movies can be used to the advantage of any teacher wanting to help students identify and understand negative stereotypes. Viewing these films can make a discussion of prejudice, bigotry, racism, and discrimination come alive. After viewing one of these movies, ask a series of questions to elicit discussion relevant to the focus of the movie. Many of the discussion questions recommended in other activities in this book would be appropriate here.

As a follow-up to the movie viewing, have the students write reviews of the movie.

Films Dealing with People with Disabilities

All God's Children	Butterflies are Free
A Patch of Blue	Coming Home
A Day in the Life of Bonnie Consolo	Circle of Children
	Sunrise
Sybil	Three Faces of Eve
If You Could See What I Hear	Who Are the Debolts?
Elephant Man	Miracle Worker
Born on the 4th of July	Children of a Lesser God
Forest Gump	My Left Foot
Rain Man	The Best Years of Our Lives
To Kill a Mockingbird	Time Bandits

Films Dealing with Cultural Differences

Zoot Suit	Ghandi
West Side Story	Fiddler on the Roof
My Fair Lady	Roots
Guess Who's Coming to Dinner	To Sir, With Love

Hotel Rwanda	Chariots of Fire
Shindler's List	Murder in Mississippi
Malcolm X	Mississippi Masala
The Third Man	Little Big Man

Films Dealing with Aging

On Golden Pond	Tribute
Sunshine Boys	Going in Style
Rhapsody in August	Cocoon
Awakenings	Driving Miss Daisy
Picture of Dorian Gray	The Bucket List

Films Dealing with Gender Differences

Nine to Five	Billy Elliott
Kramer vs. Kramer	Brokeback Mountain
Unmarried Woman	Erin Brokovich
Personal Best	Milk
Childrens Hour	Henry and June
The Crying Game	

Making the Commitment to Change*

Purpose:

This activity gives students an opportunity to join thousands of other people in pledging to stamp out racial prejudice.

Materials:

one copy of "The Birmingham Pledge" for each student; news photos, articles and books depicting the demonstrations and violence in Birmingham, Alabama, in the early 1960s (information is available on the internet)

Directions:

Read the following account of the racial violence in Birmingham and the changes that have taken place in that community since the 1950s. Present the material in your own words, using photos, news articles and other relevant materials as visual aids.

The Civil Rights Movement of the 1950s and '60s thrust Birmingham, Alabama, into the national spotlight as a scene of bitter racial conflict. Photographs of Dr. Martin Luther King behind bars, of the bombed-out Sixteenth Street Baptist Church, and of firehoses and police dogs set upon peaceful marchers remain icons of the period, indelibly linking Birmingham with hate.

The image — and the reality — of racist violence on their city streets confronted Birmingham residents with a complicated crisis. For Black citizens, the dream of participating in democracy was on the line. In the view of many Whites, including most city officials, an old and cherished concentration of power was in jeopardy. Some Whites actively supported the African American community's appeal for justice. But for one group — downtown merchants — the moral and political tensions presented an economic emergency, as well: Shoppers' fears had left the city's commercial district a ghost town.

Early efforts at renewing downtown Birmingham played primarily on this economic angle, but a few business leaders recognized the need to heal old wounds that recent events had opened. After years of working behind the scenes, with the strong urging of Black leaders the group "went public" in 1969 to establish the biracial Community Affairs Committee (CAC), under the sponsorship of an older organization called Operation New Birmingham.

Now, many years later, the CAC — comprising business, civic and religious leaders — meets every Monday morning at the Birmingham Civil

Rights Institute to discuss community concerns and to develop concrete ways of bringing the races together. The group's latest project is the Birmingham Pledge.

Since its introduction at the city's annual Martin Luther King Unity Breakfast in January, 1998, the Pledge has gathered thousands of signatures in Birmingham, as well as across the U.S. and around the world. President and Mrs. Clinton and numerous other dignitaries are among the signers. The participation of young people is especially critical in the effort to stamp out racial prejudice and discord, and the Pledge sponsors have been impressed with the commitment exhibited by students who choose to add their name.

Distribute copies of the Birmingham Pledge and read it with the students. Explain that by signing the Birmingham Pledge, they will be joining a national campaign that began as a simple vision of hope for one community. Tell them that you will make copies of their signed pledges and will send the originals to the CAC, where they will be placed in a registry at the Birmingham Civil Rights Institute.

Name a final date for return of the signed pledges, allowing several days for students to discuss the pledge with their parents if they so desire. Do not in any way pressure or single out students who fail to sign a pledge. Send collected pledges to:

Birmingham Pledge
2829 2nd Avenue South
Birmingham, AL 35233

Note: Students may also sign the pledge online at the web site of Operation New Birmingham <http://www.birminghampledge.org>.

* This entire activity is adapted and reprinted by permission from "A Commitment to Change: A City Seeks to Heal Its History of Racial Violence" © *1999, Teaching Tolerance*, Southern Poverty Law Center, Montgomery, Alabama.

Extension:

Have the students read Dr. King's 1963 "Letter from Birmingham City Jail" (available on the internet). Use the reading as a basis for discussion.

The Birmingham Pledge
Sign It. Live It.

I believe that every person has worth as an individual.

I believe that every person is entitled to dignity and respect, regardless of race or color.

I believe that every thought and every act of racial prejudice is harmful; if it is my thought or act, then it is harmful to me as well as to others.

Therefore, from this day forward I will strive daily to eliminate racial prejudice from my thoughts and actions.

I will discourage racial prejudice by others at every opportunity.

I will treat all people with dignity and respect; and I will strive daily to honor this pledge, knowing that the world will be a better place because of my effort.

_____
Signature

_____
Please print name

_____
Street address

_____
City/State Zip Code

_____
School/Organization (optional)   Date

A project of the Community Affairs Committee of Operation New Birmingham. www.birminghampledge.org

Building A Caring Community
Cooperation and Team Building

...And Justice for All

Purpose:

To understand the meaning of justice and to realize that this applies to *all* people.

Materials:

newspapers, white construction paper, colored markers, and pencils or paints

Directions:

Begin by reminding the students of the last phrase of the "Pledge of Allegiance" which says, "with liberty and justice for all." Ask the students if they know the meaning of the word *justice*. Allow volunteers to share their knowledge and perceptions of what justice is. Explain that justice means that everyone gets equal treatment under the laws of our country. It means giving deserved rewards and punishments impartially. It also means not favoring one person over another or showing prejudice against a person. On a personal level, it means treating people fairly and without prejudice or favoritism. It means respecting each other's differences and acting reasonably toward one another.

Give examples of justice at home, in the classroom, in the community, and in the nation. Share some examples from newspaper articles, and offer some personal examples as well, such as:

- All the children at home must do their chores before watching TV or going outside to play. No one is favored.
- Everyone gets a turn to talk when there is a class discussion.
- If an adult runs a red light while driving a car, that person is breaking the law and, no matter who he or she is, will have to pay a fine if caught.
- Everyone in our country who is accused of committing a crime is entitled to a fair trial.

Distribute art supplies and ask the students to think of an example of justice at home, at school, in the community, or in the nation. Invite the students to draw a picture of that example of justice. Under the picture, have them write the words. "This is an example of justice because..." completing the sentence with a brief explanation of how the picture depicts an example of justice. For example, a student might draw a picture of a child holding up a test with an "A" on it, writing below: "This is an example of justice because an 'A' is earned only by people who do well on the test."

When the pictures are finished, invite the students to show them to the class, reading aloud the reason why each is an example of justice. Post the pictures on a bulletin board in the class or in a highly visible location elsewhere in the school. Summarize the activity by asking questions and facilitating discussion.

Discussion Questions:

1. What would it be like if the teacher gave good grades only to his/her favorite students and not to everyone who earned them?
2. Why is it so difficult for us to treat each other fairly?
3. What does it mean to be partial?
4. When is it okay to be partial to someone or something? When is it not okay?
5. What is the difference between being partial and being prejudiced?
6. A popular saying states that "justice is blind." What does that mean? Do you think justice in our country is really blind?

> Justice cannot be for one side alone, but must be for both.
>
> Eleanor Roosevelt

How It Feels To Be Left Out

Purpose:

Students develop empathy by putting themselves in the place of someone who has been rejected or excluded and attempting to understand the feelings that these experiences generate.

Materials:

writing materials

Directions:

Explain to the students that you would like them to write about the topic, "How It Feels to Be Left Out." Emphasize that they will need to use their imaginations, because they are going to write from the viewpoint of a person of a different race or culture, or a person with a disability.

In your own words, explain to the students: *Imagine a situation in which a person might be excluded. Think about how you feel when you are left out of a group or activity in which you really want to participate. How might the situation and/or the feelings, be the same or different for someone of a different race or culture, or someone with a disability? If the feelings would be about the same, what would they be? If the feelings would be different, how would they be different, and what would they be like? You might begin your story when the person is just starting to think about joining the group or activity. Describe what happens that leads to the rejection, and concentrate on the expression of feelings throughout.*

Ask the students to indicate at the end of their papers whether or not they would be willing to read their story to the class. Collect the papers and evaluate them in your usual manner, then return them to the students. Ask volunteers to read their stories to the class. Facilitate a discussion after each reading, basing your questions on issues presented in the story. Conclude the activity with a general discussion.

Discussion Questions:

1. *How are the feelings of most people the same in response to rejection? How are they different for people who belong to a minority race or culture? ... for people who have a disability?*
2. *What did you discover about your own attitudes towards people who belong to minorities or have disabilities?*
3. *What good does it do to try to understand each other's feelings?*
4. *What new ideas did you get about rejecting others? ... about handling rejection? ... about the idea of inclusion?*

The Clique Phenomenon

Purpose:

The students will identify ways to make new friends and understand the effects of cliques on those left out. They will also develop and follow through on a plan to make at least one new friend.

Materials:

whiteboard or chart paper; the experience sheet, "Getting On Your Own Side," one copy for each student

Directions:

Have the students form two teams. Give the teams 10 to 15 minutes to brainstorm a list describing as many ways as they can think of to make new friends. At the end of the allotted time, reconvene the class and ask the groups to share their lists. Possible ideas include:

- Sit beside someone different in the cafeteria and say hello.
- Offer to show someone new around the school.
- Join a school organization.
- Offer to help someone carry a heavy load.
- Team up with someone you don't know very well to work on a class project.
- Run an ad in the school paper asking for a companion for particular activities, like hiking or bicycling.
- Ask someone you know to introduce you to new people.
- Go to the gym or track after school and say hello to the kids who are practicing.

Write the word *clique* on the board and ask the students to help you define it. One possible definition might be:

An in-group or gang of kids that defines itself as much by who is excluded as by who is included.

Discuss how a clique's policy of exclusion causes members to have difficulty making new friends, and can completely frustrate the efforts of someone who is not in the clique to become good friends with someone who is. Stress that the reason many kids want to be a part of a clique is that they want to be liked by "important" people and feel important themselves. Also point out that generally cliques consist of people from the same cultural, ethnic or racial backgrounds. Cliques usually exclude anyone "different" from their members.

Ask the students to turn to the experience sheet, "Getting On Your Own Side." Allow the students about 10 minutes to complete the sheet. Then ask them to rejoin their teams and (voluntarily) share their answers to the questions.

Encourage the students to commit to making one new friend in the next week or including one new person in their existing group of friends. Explain that this assignment carries one important restriction: The person they befriend or include in their group should be different from them (or the group) in some way.

Stipulate that before they can claim to have completed the assignment, the students must do something tangible with the new friend, such as sit together at an assembly, eat lunch together, go jogging or bicycling together, visit each other's home, see a movie together, or play video games after school. Ask the students to pay particular attention to the "clique phenomenon" and avoid doing anything that causes another person to feel left out. Conclude the activity with a discussion.

Discussion Questions:

1. *In what ways do you think cliques are good?*
2. *In what ways do you think cliques are harmful?*
3. *In what ways do the members of a clique miss out when they exclude others that are different from them?*
4. *Of what value to a group is having varied membership?*
5. *Have you ever wanted to belong to a clique? If so, why was it important?*
6. *What would happen if there were no cliques at this school?*
7. *What kinds of cliques do adults have?*

Extension:

An excellent follow up to this activity is the Sharing Circle, "When Someone Made Me Feel Like Part of the Group," on page 103.

It's not easy being green.

Kermit The Frog

Getting on Your Own Side
Experience Sheet

Is it worth it to be in?

What have you done to be included In a group?

I have...

  __Yes__No   ●   risked losing friends.

  __Yes__No   ●   hurt people who thought they were my friends by making them feel left out.

  __Yes__No   ●   done something I thought was not right.

  __Yes__No   ●   done something I knew was against the law.

  __Yes__No   ●   drunk alcohol or used drugs.

  __Yes__No   ●   done something that might have harmed me physically.

  __Yes__No   ●   done something that cost me a lot of money.

  __Yes__No   ●   done something that interfered with my school work.

  __Yes__No   ●   done something my parents would have objected to if they had known.

  __Yes__No   ●   done whatever was necessary, as long as it didn't harm anyone else.

  __Yes__No   ●   done something that was against my religion.

  __Yes__No   ●   done whatever was necessary.

Can you remember a time when you were pressured to exclude someone from an activity?

How did you feel?

What did you do?

If this ever happens again, what do you think you will do?

Connect!

Purpose:

As students cooperate in solving a problem, they begin to identify specific cooperative and competitive behaviors. Later they are asked to describe how those behaviors affected completion of the task.

Note: The crucial element in this game is that players, through their actions, may freely offer and give puzzle pieces to other members of their team, but they may not ask for or take puzzle pieces. Since the entire game is played silently, the player who "gets it" will carefully observe other players and offer them pieces she or he has that they need. If this modeling is successful, soon all players will be sharing puzzle pieces and all of the puzzles will be quickly completed. The role of the observer is extremely important because once the game really gets going, players in their enthusiasm will be tempted to start snatching pieces and using hand gestures to "ask for" pieces, behaviors that are strictly forbidden.

Materials:

construction paper or tag board (one color only) with which to make a set of puzzle pieces for each group of players; table and chairs for each group of players

Directions:

Start with eight 8-inch by 8-inch squares of construction paper or tag board *for each team.* Individually cut each square into three to five smaller pieces (see illustration). Place all of the pieces for one team in a single envelope.

If the entire class is playing, ask the students to form teams of five to eight. Have each team sit around a table, and select one member to be its observer. Announce that all other team members are players.

Take the observers aside and say to them: *Your job is to stand beside the table while your team is playing the game and notice what happens. Be prepared to describe such things as how well the group works together, who shares puzzle parts and who does not; whether members concentrate only on the puzzle in front of them or watch the progress of all the puzzles; cooperative vs. competitive behaviors; any conflicts that occur and how they are resolved.*

Read aloud the following rules of play:
- Your task is to assemble eight squares of EQUAL size.
- There will be NO talking, pointing, or other nonverbal communication.

- A player may pass puzzle parts to any other team member at any time.
- You may NOT take, ask for, or indicate in any way that you want another team member's puzzle pieces.
- There is no time limit (or you may choose to determine a specific length of time).

Distribute the puzzle pieces randomly among the players. Give each player approximately the same number of pieces.

Give the signal to start play.

At the conclusion of play, have the observers give feedback to their team. If several teams are playing, have the observers do this simultaneously. Advise the teams to listen carefully, and not to interrupt, argue with, or put down the observer in any way.

Discussion Questions:

1. *What did you learn from your observer?*
2. *What was the object of the game?*
3. *Which kind of behavior was most effective in this game, cooperative or competitive? Why?*
4. *What are some of the differences between cooperation and competition?*
5. *What are some of the effects of competitive behavior on a team? ...of cooperative behavior?*
6. *If you could play the game again, how would you change your own behavior?*
7. *What did you learn from this experience?*

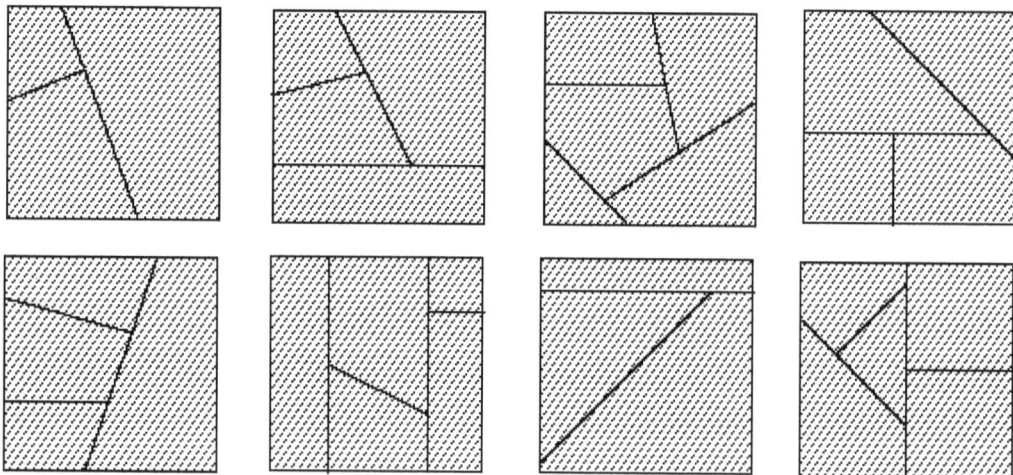

Extending the Learning— Sharing Circles

Sharing Circle Guidelines

The Sharing Circle is a unique small-group discussion process in which members follow an established procedure and adhere to a few basic rules as they talk about a specific topic. Topics facilitate growth by encouraging sharing, awareness, self-disclosure, mutual acceptance, and positive interaction.

What makes the Sharing Circle a powerful tool for teaching tolerance and respect for differences is that its structure, procedure, and rules assure every individual equal time, equal consideration, and equal respect and, as implied in the title, Sharing Circles are conducted in *circles*. This arrangement gives every member a position of equality and creates face to face dialogue.

Goals of the Sharing Circle

All Sharing Circles share a set of general goals that relate to the development and expression of intrapersonal and interpersonal excellence. These are goals of *every* circle, no matter what the topic. In a sense, they are *prerequisite* goals. Through their attainment the students are empowered to achieve the more specific goals implied by the circle' topic or objective.

General Goals

- To open avenues of communication
- To build trust and understanding
- To develop awareness of self and others
- To develop positive interaction skills
- To encourage quality listening, and the use of other communication skills
- To develop empathy

Developing Individual and Group Awareness

Our emotional and intellectual lives are so complex that we would be devastated if we couldn't discuss our experiences with one another. When we engage in self-observation and contemplation, and then share our thoughts and feelings at a level beyond superficiality, we develop self-awareness. We come to understand ourselves by looking inward and recognizing how we feel, think, and behave in response to people and events around us. When we listen to others do the same — all in an environment of safety — we expand our understanding of others. Upon these kinds of positive relationships and mutual understandings, a climate of tolerance and respect for individual differences develops.

Used regularly, the Sharing Circle, coupled with its *content* (specific discussion topics), provides the students with frequent opportunities to observe themselves and others in action, and to begin seeing how they contribute to the culture of the group. Students and teachers alike become *real people* to each other. Even among students who you thought had nothing in common a likely outcome is an exposing of an underlying humanity that erases superficial differences and leads to mutual respect.

Encouraging Group Interaction

Relating effectively to others is a challenge all students face. The Sharing Circle brings out and affirms the positive qualities inherent in everyone and allows participants to practice effective modes of communication.

One of the greatest benefits of the Sharing Circle is that it gently forces students to positively and respectfully interact regardless of what diversity initially separates them. Every Sharing Circle is a real-life experience where students share, listen, explore, plan, and problem solve together. As they interact, they learn about each other and come to realize what it takes to relate effectively to other people.

Positive interaction skills are developed through observing how others feel, think, and behave and comparing these observations to their own feelings, thoughts, and behaviors. These comparisons are the antecedents of empathy. Students begin to recognize what is effective — what works and doesn't work. They identify what others want and need from them and to value the *positive* effects that they can have on others.

The Power of Listening

The Sharing Circle provides students with many opportunities to talk while others actively listen. Listening is perhaps the most powerful interaction skill that can be developed. Just through the consistent process of sharing in a safe environment, students develop the ability to clarify their thoughts and are encouraged to go deeper and to become more self-aware.

Many people do not realize that merely listening can be immensely facilitating to the personal development of others. We do not need to diagnose, probe, or problem solve to help students focus attention on their own needs and use the information and insights in their own minds to arrive at their own conclusions. Because being listened to gives students confidence in their ability to positively affect their lives, listening is certainly the communication skill with the greatest long-term payoff. Listening communicates two messages: understanding and acceptance.

How the Sharing Circle Works

Life is full of rules, and the Sharing Circle is no exception. Characteristically, students learn to take the rules of the circle very seriously. They are neither difficult to follow nor a threat to anyone's personal style. In fact, by assuring safety, equality, and inclusion, the rules of the Sharing Circle actually remove many hidden roadblocks to communication and enjoyment. As students participate in Sharing Circles, they find them to be an enjoyable and valuable experience in part because of the safe environment created by the rules. In a group's first few circles, it helps to take time to go over the rules and elaborate a bit on each one. Once the circle is smoothly operational, stating the rules is usually no longer necessary. The behavior of the students demonstrates the presence of the rules with striking clarity.

Sharing Circle Rules

- Listen to the person speaking without interrupting or probing.
- Respect all comments.
- Share the time equally.
- Allow everyone a turn to speak.
- Speak or pass — the choice is yours.

Most of the rules are self-explanatory. Listening means *really* listening, not mentally rehearsing what you are going to say, not daydreaming. All members of the group receive equal acceptance and respect as do, by extension, their contributions. Since time is usually limited, mentally calculate about how much time each student has to share and let them know how much time to take when sharing. As the leader, you will determine how much time to devote to each session. Smaller groups (8-12) are easier to manage and assure everyone's turn. Remind the students that no one is going to interrupt them; therefore, it is their responsibility to stop so that the next person can have his or her turn. If a student does begin to monopolize the allocated time, gently remind him or her to finish their thought and then go on to another student. Allow every member of the group the opportunity to speak to the topic at least once. Assure them that they will never be coerced or pressured to speak, but that their turn is an absolute given right.

It is the responsibility of the teacher or counselor (as leader) to introduce the topic, and to ensure that the students adhere to the Sharing Procedure and follow the rules. As the leader, you will need to remain aware of time constraints so that the entire circle can be completed without curtailing anyone's right to speak.

Sharing Procedure

- Make sure the ground rules are understood by all students.
- Introduce the topic.
- Elaborate on the topic.
- Allow time for members to share their thoughts.
- Lead a general discussion so that students have an opportunity to talk about learnings and insights.

Elaborating on a topic simply means giving examples and perhaps defining a term or two, so that everyone understands what is expected. Examples demonstrate the value of sharing *specific* ideas or thoughts, as opposed to generalizations. Every topic in this book is provided with an elaboration sample. You do not need to read this elaboration verbatim, but rather, take the ideas presented and put them into your own words.

Once the topic has been introduced and elaborated upon by the leader, there are two distinct phases to each Sharing Circle. The first part is the sharing phase, and the second is the general discussion in response to questions asked by the leader. This discussion phase provides an opportunity for the students to focus on what they are learning from participation in the circle.

Perhaps the trickiest distinction to make as a new leader involves the differences between the sharing and discussion phases of the circle. These two phases are procedurally and qualitatively different, yet of equal importance. During the sharing phase, students and the leader voluntarily share their feelings, ideas, and insights concerning the topic. Each person is given an uninterrupted turn while everyone else listens. Only after *all members* who choose to share have done so, does the leader ask questions and open up the circle to the give and take of general discussion. The longer you participate in Sharing Circles, the more you will appreciate the benefits of maintaining the integrity of these two phases. Each Sharing Circle in this book is provided with several discussion questions. Use any or all of these questions to stimulate discussion or you may also ask your own questions.

Something I Enjoy About Another Culture

Purpose:

In this circle students recognize and discuss the multicultural nature of our society and describe customs, beliefs and practices of various contributing cultures.

Introduce the topic:

Our topic today is, "Something I Enjoy About Another Culture." When we talk about a culture we mean the beliefs, history, practices, customs, arts and other things produced by a group of people. In our country, we have one big culture, the U.S. culture, made up of many contributing cultures with roots in the past or in other nations, such as the native American Indian nations, Africa, Mexico, Japan, Vietnam, China, Germany, Israel, and many more. Thus, we sometimes refer to the African-American culture, the Mexican-American culture, the Native American culture, or the Japanese-American culture.

Tell us something you like and appreciate about a contributing culture different from your own. Think about such things as food, music, art, religion, costumes, poetry, dance, books, and any customs you know about, such as the way holidays, weddings or birthdays are celebrated. Think it over for a few moments. The topic is, "Something I Enjoy About Another Culture."

Discussion Questions:

1. *What cultural customs or practices were mentioned in this session that you'd like to learn more about?*
2. *Why is it important for us to respect and learn from the many cultures that contribute to our common culture?*
3. *How can we show respect and tolerance for other cultures in our daily lives?*

A Member of My Cultural Group Whom I Admire

Purpose:

This circle gives students an opportunity to explore the values, attitudes and beliefs of their cultures by focusing on individuals who are strong, positive representatives of those cultures.

Introduce the topic:

Today, we're going to talk about individual representatives of our cultures who are important to us in some way. The topic is, "A Member of My Cultural Group Whom I Admire."

Think of someone of the same cultural group as you whom you admire and respect. This person does not need to be famous. She or he can be someone older than you, the same age or even younger. You may not even know this person very well. However, based on what you do know, the feelings you have are those of respect and admiration. Perhaps the person's lifestyle fits your image of the way you want to live. Maybe something about his or her personality impresses you. Or it could be that this is a well known person who stands for values that you believe in. Think about what makes you look up to someone of your own culture. The topic is, "A Member of My Cultural Group Whom I Admire."

Discussion Questions:

1. *Did you notice any similarities in the people we mentioned? If so, what were they?*
2. *Do you think most of us try to be like people from our own cultural groups? Why or why not?*
3. *In what ways are you a representative of your culture?*

Something I Like About Myself That Is Part of Me Because of My Culture

Purpose:

This topic encourages students to openly express pride in their cultures and in themselves as members and products of those cultures.

Introduce the topic:

Today's topic is, "Something I Like About Myself That Is Part of Me Because of My Culture." In this session you are encouraged to brag a little about specific characteristics in yourself that are related to your culture. If you have a hard time saying nice things about yourself, this may seem like a tough topic, but please give it a try.

Take some time to think of ways in which your culture has influenced you to become the individual you are today. Maybe the influence of your culture can be seen in your choice of clothes, lifestyle, music or leisure activities, such as the TV shows you watch or the way you dance. Perhaps you are bilingual and proud of your ability to speak two languages. Or maybe you are proud of something deeper like your character or your values. Take a minute to think about it and then tell us your thoughts. The topic is, "Something I Like About Myself That Is Part of Me Because of My Culture."

Discussion Questions:

1. *What new or surprising information did you learn about one or more members of the group?*
2. *We were proud of different things, but did you notice any similarities in the way we felt?*
3. *How important do you think cultural influences are in our lives?*

Something I Respect About a Person of a Different Race or Culture

Purpose:

This circle asks students to identify the basis for the respect they feel for someone of a different race or culture, and provides an opportunity to demonstrate tolerance for people with different beliefs and practices.

Introduce the topic:

Our topic today is, "Something I Respect About a Person of a Different Race or Culture." This is a topic that will probably take a little thought. The person you choose to talk about can be someone you know personally or someone you don't know but have heard about. The important thing is that you have a feeling of respect for this person. I'd like you to explore the reasons behind that respect.

For example, maybe you have a neighbor who is of a different race and you respect him because he is friendly and helpful to everyone who lives on your street. Or perhaps someone in your family married a person from a different culture and you respect her because she is very smart, or very funny, or very understanding. Maybe you've heard or read about the leader of another nation, and you respect that person's ideas about how to have peace in the world. Or maybe you know about the head of an organization or cultural group who is an exceptional leader. Remember that respect can be earned in small ways, too. Maybe you respect this person for something as simple as showing pride in his or her culture. Take a few moments to consider the topic. It is, "Something I Respect About a Person of a Different Race or Culture."

Discussion Questions:

1. *Why do people have such different ideas? Why do we do things so differently?*
2. *What can you learn from people who have different beliefs and customs than you have?*
3. *What is tolerance?*
4. *How can you become a more tolerant person?*

What I Think Good Communication Is

Purpose:

In this circle, students will have an opportunity to identify specific components and benefits of effective communication.

Introduce the topic:

Today's topic for discussion is, "What I Think Good Communication Is." Communication is an exchange of thoughts, feelings, opinions and/or information between two or more people. Today we're going to focus on the ingredients of good communication. There are no right or wrong answers; whatever you contribute will help us develop a better understanding of what's involved. If you like, try thinking about a person with whom you've had success communicating and tell us some of the things that happen during your interactions with that person. Take a few minutes and then we'll begin sharing on our topic, "What I Think Good Communication Is."

Discussion Questions:

1. *What quality or ingredient of good communication was mentioned most often during our sharing?*
2. *Why is it important to practice good communication?*
3. *How can good communication help promote understanding and tolerance?*

I Time I Listened Well

Purpose:

This circle asks the students to describe times when they listened effectively and to identify effective listening behaviors.

Introduce the topic:

Most of us appreciate having someone really listen to us. In this session we are going to turn this idea around and talk about how it feels to listen to someone else. The topic is, "A Time I Listened Well."

Can you remember a time when you really paid attention to someone and listened carefully to what he or she said? This means that you didn't interrupt with your own ideas or daydream about your own plans, but really concentrated and tried to understand what the other person was attempting to get across. Maybe you've listened to a friend like that, or a younger brother or sister, or a teacher or coach. Think about it for a few moments and, if you wish, tell us about, "A Time I Listened Well."

Discussion Questions:

1. *What kinds of things make listening difficult?*
2. *Why is it important to listen to others?*
3. *What could you do to improve your listening?*
4. *How do you feel when someone really listens to you?*

I Got Into a Conflict

Purpose:

Students are asked to describe conflicts they have experienced and what caused them. In so doing, they examine strategies for resolving conflict and ways of dealing with the feelings conflict generates.

Introduce the topic:

Our topic today is, "I Got Into a Conflict." Conflicts are very common. They occur because of big and little things that happen in our lives. And sometimes the smallest things that happen can lead to the biggest conflicts. This is your opportunity to talk about a time when you had an argument or fight with someone. Maybe you and a friend argued over something that one of you said that the other didn't like. Or maybe you argued with a brother or sister over what TV show to watch, or who should do a particular chore around the house. Have you ever had a fight because someone broke a promise or couldn't keep a secret? If you feel comfortable telling us what happened, we'd like to hear it. Describe what the other person did and said, and what you did and said. Tell us how you felt and how the other person seemed to feel. There's just one thing you shouldn't tell us and that's the name of the other person, okay? Take a few moments to think about it. The topic is, "I Got Into a Conflict."

Discussion Questions:

1. *How did most of us feel when we were part of a conflict?*
2. *What kinds of things led to the conflicts that we shared?*
3. *How could some of our conflicts have been prevented?*
4. *What conflict management strategies could have been used in the situations that we shared?*

How I Handled a Disagreement With a Friend

Purpose:

In this circle the students will describe conflict situations involving their peers and explain strategies used to resolve those conflicts.

Introduce the topic:

All of us at one time or another have probably disagreed with a friend and had negative feelings as a result. So today let's talk about those times. Our topic is, "How I Handled a Disagreement With a Friend."

The disagreement you describe may have been a major thing that led to the end of the friendship or it may have been resolved in such a way that your friendship became even stronger. You can describe a disagreement that happened to you and a friend when you were children, or one that occurred very recently. The disagreement may have built up over a long period, or it may have been a one-of-a-kind situation that cropped up very suddenly. Try to recreate in your mind what happened and, without telling us the name of your friend, describe the situation and what you did. The topic is, "How I Handled a Disagreement With a Friend."

Discussion Questions:

1. *What are the most common feelings that disagreements generate?*
2. *What were some of the main differences you noticed in the situations described?*
3. *How do you usually respond to disagreements?*
4. *What strategies did you learn from this session that will help you handle future disagreements?*

How I Learned to Get Along With Someone Who Doesn't Think The Way I Do

Purpose:

This circle enables students to recognize that they know and get along with many people who don't think the way they do, and to realize that their own values need not change because of the people around them.

Introduce the topic:

We've all had jobs or taken classes where we've had to get along with people whose ideas and ways of thinking are different from ours. Today we're going to talk about some of these times. Our topic is, "How I Learned to Get Along With Someone Who Doesn't Think the Way I Do."

Differences in thinking are quite common among company employees, classmates and members of teams, clubs or other organizations. The differences can arise from cultural and family traditions, language preferences, political views and lots of other things, but they become most striking when they surface during a conflict of some kind. Think of a situation like this in your life and tell us what has helped you to get along with this person? Do you constantly hide your feelings and thoughts? Do you try to get your own way by using tricks or playing mind games? Or have the two of you learned to accept each other? If you decide to share, tell us what works for you and how you feel about it. Our topic is, "How I Learned to Get Along With Someone Who Doesn't Think the Way I Do."

Discussion Questions:

1. *Is it worth the effort to learn to get along with people who think differently? What are the benefits?*
2. *What would it be like if we could only associate with people whose values and beliefs were exactly like ours?*
3. *What are some of the techniques we use to get along with people who think differently?*

A Time I Was Rejected Because Something About Me Was Different

Purpose:

This circle is designed to help students become more aware of how it feels to be rejected for something over which they have no control.

Introduce the topic:

Our topic for today's session is "A Time I Was Rejected Because Something About Me Was Different." Our purpose for discussing this topic is to find out how things like this happen and to talk about how it feels to be left out or turned away for something that you can't or won't change. So think of a time when this happened to you. What was it about you that led to the rejection? Was it the color of your skin? Were you too tall or not tall enough? Perhaps your clothing was unacceptable to the person or group who rejected you. Or maybe it was your weight, language or a disability. If you decide to share, tell us what happened without telling us who rejected you. The topic is, "I Was Rejected Because Something About Me Was Different."

Discussion Questions:

1. *How are people affected when they are rejected for something about them that's different?*
2. *How are incidents like this related to prejudice?*
3. *Why are we afraid or suspicious of differences among people?*
4. *What can we do to become more accepting of differences?*

A Way I Show Tolerance

Purpose:

This circle prompts students to describe examples of tolerant behavior and to recognize that a multicultural society includes people of different beliefs who have different ways of doing things.

Introduce the topic:

Tolerance is a very important word in our language. It also conveys a very important idea. Tolerance means recognizing and accepting the beliefs and practices of others, especially when they are different from our own. Today we're going to talk about what it means to recognize and accept another person's beliefs and ways of doing things. Our topic is, "A Way I Show Tolerance."

How do you show your friends, classmates and family members that it's okay with you if they have different beliefs than you have, and do things in different ways? When someone says something you don't agree with, do you listen carefully and see what you can learn? Maybe you say something like, "That's your opinion, but I have a different one," or "That's interesting," or "Let me see if I understand you." Or perhaps you just remain quiet and don't say anything. Think about this carefully. Our topic is, "A Way I Show Tolerance."

Discussion Questions:

1. *Can you think of anything you do every day that couldn't be done in a different way?*
2. *Why do people get into arguments and fights over the "right" answer or the "right" way of doing something?*
3. *Why is it important to show tolerance for the beliefs and practices of others?*

A Time I Was Stereotyped

Purpose:

This circle is designed to help students develop a greater awareness of what stereotyping is and how people feel when they are viewed or treated through the lens of a stereotype.

Introduce the topic:

Today's topic is, "A Time I Was Stereotyped." Remember, a stereotype is an oversimplified image or concept that a lot of people buy into. We've all seen examples of stereotyping on TV, and you've probably seen it many times in your daily lives. Sometimes people are cast in a stereotyped role and they're not even aware of it.

See if you can think of a time when you are sure someone stereotyped you. They decided what kind of a person you were without really getting to know you as an individual. Perhaps it was an isolated incident or maybe it's something that happens all the time. What do you think contributed to the stereotyping? Your appearance? Mannerisms? Accent? Or was it just ignorance on the part of the other person? What were your feelings when it happened? If you decide to share, describe the incident and how you felt without telling us the name of the person who stereotyped you. The topic is "A Time I Was Stereotyped."

Discussion Questions:

1. *What does stereotyping do to its victims on the inside? How does it affect the person who is doing the stereotyping?*
2. *Why do we generalize about people and put them in categories instead of viewing them as individuals?*
3. *What can you do to discourage stereotyping when it occurs?*

I Judged a Person Based on Looks Alone

Purpose:

In this circle, the students have the opportunity to examine prejudiced opinions they formed, define the term *stereotyping,* and explain why judgments based on outward appearances are unreliable.

Introduce the topic:

Today our topic is, "I Judged a Person Based on Looks Alone." It may not be fair, but this is something we all do from time to time. See if you can think of an example from your own experience that you'd be willing to share. Maybe you felt disgusted when you saw a fat woman, or were uneasy when you passed a raggedly dressed man on the street. Perhaps you assumed that someone couldn't speak English, just from the color of his skin. Or maybe you had someone pegged as a rich snob just because she drove a fancy car. Have you ever had a negative impression upon seeing someone and later discovered that he was really nice? Have you been attracted to someone, and later found out that she was self-centered or boring? Think back and see if you can recall an instance like this. Tell us what you concluded about the person and why. And if you changed your opinion later, explain what influenced you. The topic is, "I Judged a Person Based on Looks Alone"

Discussion Questions:

1. *What is meant by the term* stereotyping? *Was what you did a form of stereotyping? Was it a form of prejudice? Explain.*
2. *What causes people to have prejudiced reactions to others?*
3. *What's dangerous about "judging a book by its cover?"*
4. *How can you keep yourself from formulating snap judgments?*

I Was Labeled Based on Something I Couldn't Change

Purpose:

This circle gives students an opportunity to describe how they responded to situations in which they were stereotyped by labeling language, and to identify ways to discourage the practice of labeling others.

Introduce the topic:

One of the problems with labels — even flattering labels — is that they limit people. They cause us to see the labeled person as whatever the label says rather than as a complex, unique individual. Today we're going to talk about our own experiences with being labeled and how those labels caused us to feel and react. Our topic is, "I Was Labeled Based on Something I Couldn't Change." Think of a time when someone, or a group of people, labeled you. Maybe the label had to do with your appearance, your scholastic or athletic ability — or lack of it — or your racial or religious background. People get stuck with labels based on problem complexions, hair color, height, weight, facial features — even the size of their feet. We even label people for things that happened years ago or things other members of their families did. Think of a label that you're dealing with now or one that you carried in the past. Tell us how you feel about that label and the effect it has had on your life. Think about it for a few moments. The topic is, "I Was Labeled Based on Something I Couldn't Change."

Discussion Questions:

1. *How did most of us react to being labeled?*
2. *Why do we label people? What purpose does it serve?*
3. *What can you do to discourage your peers from labeling one another?*
4. *What can you do to influence adults who thoughtlessly or maliciously use labels?*

When Someone Made Me Feel Like Part of the Group

Purpose:

This circle is designed to help students recognize that feeling like a stranger or outsider is not uncommon, and that they can help others experience the positive feeling of being welcomed and included.

Introduce the topic:

Today our topic is, "When Someone Made Me Feel Like Part of the Group." Most of us have had the experience of being an outsider. Usually this happens when we are new to an area or school or when we are around new people. Most of us probably don't like the uncomfortable feeling of being left out and of wanting to be included. Think of a time when you felt this way and someone took the time to get to know you, introduced you to the group and made you feel welcome. That person was your ticket to being "in." Maybe it happened at a club meeting or a dance. Or perhaps you were living in a new neighborhood or had just enrolled in a new school. Describe the specific situation, and tell us about the person who made you feel welcome and wanted. Our topic is, "A Time Someone Made Me Feel Like Part of the Group."

Discussion Questions:

1. *What kinds of behaviors help people feel accepted?*
2. *How would you go about helping someone feel like part of your group?*
3. *How does it affect a group or organization when members really identify with the group and feel like they belong?*

We Made Room for One More

Purpose:

This circle invites students to describe how they responded to someone's desire to be included, and to discuss the need of people to belong and be accepted.

Introduce the topic:

Today we're going to talk about inclusion and exclusion. Our topic is, "We Made Room for One More." Think of a time when you made an effort to include someone. Maybe you and your friends found enough room in the car for an extra person who wanted to go with you to a game or party. Or perhaps you knew someone who really wanted to be part of an organization or group you belong to, and you made an effort to get that person involved. How did you feel? Was this an easy thing for you to do, or did you have to pull some strings? If you had the chance to do it again, would you? Think about it for a few moments. The topic is, "We Made Room for One More."

Discussion Questions:

1. *How did the person who was included seem to feel?*
2. *How do you feel about having the power to include someone?*
3. *Why do we feel the need to belong to groups?*
4. *How does it feel to be excluded?*
5. *How can a person who is excluded most of the time learn the social skills that groups teach us?*

I Have a Friend Who Is Different From Me

Purpose:

This circle asks students to identify specific differences between themselves and their friends, and fosters respect for differences in race, culture, lifestyle and ability.

Introduce the topic:

Today we are going to talk about friends who are different from us and what we like about them. The topic for this session is, "I Have a Friend Who Is Different From Me."

We are all alike in many ways, but we are also different. Today, I want you to think about a friend who is different from you in at least one major way, and tell us why you like this person so much. Perhaps your friend is of a different race, or has a much larger family, or is many years older than you. Does your friend speak a different language or eats a different way than you do? Does your friend have a disability that causes his or her lifestyle to be different from yours? Maybe your friend celebrates birthdays differently than you do, or has different holidays. Tell us what you enjoy about this person. Does your friend listen to you and share things with you? Does he or she invite you to go places? Do you have something in common like a love of sports, music, or computers? Think about it for a few minutes. The topic is, "I Have a Friend Who Is Different From Me."

Discussion Questions:

1. *What are some of the ways we differ from our friends?*
2. *How are you enriched by the differences between you and your friend?*
3. *What causes people to dislike other people because of things like race or religion?*
4. *What would our lives be like if we could only make friends with people who are just like we are?*

A Time I Stood Up for Something I Strongly Believe In

Purpose:

This circle encourages students to describe times when they behaved assertively regarding a strongly held value or principle and to demonstrate understanding of assertive versus nonassertive behaviors.

Introduce the topic:

Many times during our lives, we are given the opportunity to speak out for the things we believe in. By now, most of us have experienced at least one such occasion. Taking a stand can be a difficult experience, especially if friends or relatives don't agree with our position. Even when they do agree, it's not necessarily easy to state our beliefs publicly. Today, we're going to talk about the conviction and determination these situations demand. Our topic is, "A Time I Stood Up for Something I Strongly Believe In."

Perhaps you saw a group of people doing something that you felt was wrong and decided that they needed to be confronted. Maybe you observed some kids teasing or harassing another kid and intervened. Or maybe, during a conversation about a controversial subject, you stated your beliefs even though everyone else in the group held the opposing view. Perhaps you decided to leave a group that was excluding kids of other races or religions, but before you left made sure that everyone knew you thought what they were doing was wrong and dangerous. One thing is generally true. When we stand up for what we believe in, we feel a sense of pride and accomplishment, and the more often we do it, the greater our courage the next time it happens. If you decide to share, please don't mention the names of other people involved. The topic is, "A Time I Stood Up for Something I Strongly Believe In."

Discussion Questions:

1. *As you look back on the situation you shared, how do you feel about it right now?*
2. *Why is it sometimes hard to stand up for your beliefs?*
3. *What are the risks of taking a stand? What are the benefits?*
4. *What are some ills in our society that people need to take a stand against?*